JN438051

한국수력원자력(주)
영광원자력본부

The 27th World Poetry Kaya Golden Crown Prize Winner(2013)

The Poetic Anthology Awarded : The Social Cleanup Movement by the Satirical Sijo
수상 시집 : 풍시조로 사회정화 운동을

*Graduated from Dept. of national Language, Deoksung Women's University, and of Literary & Creative Arts of Seorabeol University of Arts, and from Dept of Public Welfare Service of Seoul Joongang Theological Seminary (University of Kannam), and from the Graduate School, University of South Carolina.
*A Member of the Literary Men's Association of Korea.
*A member of the Christian Poets' Association of Korea.
*A Member of the Female's Literary Society of Korea.
*A Member of the Modern Poet's Association.
*A Director of International Pen Club, in Korea Headquarters.

***Poetical Anthology**: The Green Field with No Dew-Laden, with other 9 vols.
***The selected Poems**: Brightening on Soul's Wick, with other 3 vols.
***The Collection of Essay**: Sivery Sands of my Life I Picked Up While Working, with other 3 vols.
***The Collection of Prayer**: Listening to my Words, ect.

*Awarded a great Prize of the Poetic Literature of Korea.
*Awarded a Prize of No-san Literature.
*Awarded a great Prize of Park Wha-mok Literature
*Awarded a great Prize of Heo-nan-sul-heon Literature, etc.

*Present: Chairman of A Juridical Person of Gawha Medical Fund.
*A Director of Choon-woo Culture Center.

* 서울덕성여대 국문과와 서라벌예대 문창과를 수료하고 서울중앙신학대학(현 강남대학교) 사회사업학과와 미국 유니버시티 사우스캐롤라이나 대학원 졸업
* 한국문인협회 회원
* 한국기독교시인협회 회원
* 한국여성문학인회 회원
* 현대시인협회 회원
* 국제펜클럽 한국본부 이사

* 시집: 이슬이 내리지 않는 초원 외 9권
* 시선집: 영혼의 심지에 불 밝혀 외 3권
* 수필집: 일하며 건져 올린 내 삶의 은빛 모래 외 3권
* 기도문집: 내 말에 귀를 기울이사 외 다수

* 한국시문학 대상
* 노산문학상
* 박화목문학 대상
* 허난설헌문학 대상 외 다수

* 현재 의료법인 가화의료재단 이사장
* 춘우문학관 관장

Winner 수상자 : Poet Jun Duk-ki 전덕기(全悳炽) 시인

A Satire's Esthetics of Pure Castigation

The poetical roles and effects depend on the castigation. The castigation, as a synonym with punishment and chastisement, has different meaning a little bit, but it means to inflict a penalty on all. And it includes from corporal punishments and monetary punishment, to labor's punishment and service's one.

Compared to the above, the satire's castigation, as a pure penalty, shares the metaphysical poetics. Here 'the pure castigation' means not the punishment by the corporal controls and physical or lawful sanctions, but a cultural punishment, namely, a poetic punishment. That is to say, this poetic punishment means to make us repent our errors through the poetic deep emotion with spiritual influence, and to experience catharsis.

Not only against the cultural calamities as the environmental pollution and ozonic destruction but also against all of the human's menace, the poetic castigation makes them able to improve only by the poetic power of the modern age or universe's.

Frequently we are liable to define this 'satire' with intention to betterment of vices, so we might use it as a target of attack to make sarcastic, to charge cynically, to defame, or slander personally, but contrary to this, the satire works the warm humanity for the betterment of vices in its back.

'Social Purification by Satiric Poetry' of Jun Duk-ki's poetical anthology, under the banner of the social campaign to purge is wielding around all of our society and so we are sure that its great outcry should be heard as a consolation of good friend of today.

<Park Jin-whan(Literary Critic, Ph.D.)>

순수한 통징의 풍시조 미학

풍시조(諷詩調)의 시적 역할과 효용은 통징(痛懲)으로 좌우된다. 통징이란 징벌이나 엄벌과 동의어로서 그 명명은 서로 달라도 다같이 벌을 주는 것을 의미한다. 그리고 벌에는 체형이나 벌금형을 비롯해 노동형, 봉사형과 같은 법적 제재나 육체적 형벌을 가하는 것들이 포함된다.

이에 비해 풍시조에서의 통징은 일종의 '순수한 통징'으로써 형이상시의 시법과 궤를 같이 한다. 여기에서 '순수한 통징'이란 육체적 제약이나 물리적, 법적 제재에 의한 징벌이 아니라 문화적 징벌 곧 시적 엄벌을 의미한다. 시적 엄벌이란 시적 감동이나 감화에 의해 잘못을 깨닫고 뉘우치게 하여 정신적 감화, 곧 카타르시스를 체험하게 하여 잘못을 개선(改善)하게 하는 문화적 수단의 징벌쯤이 된다.

뿐만 아니라 환경오염이나 오존층의 파괴를 비롯한 문명적 재해를 비롯해 핵이나 전쟁과 같은 인류위협 전반에 걸쳐 감행됨으로써 통징은 시대나 현실은 물론 우주적 시력에 의해서만 감행될 수 있는 개선이라고 하는 악의 교정에 해당되게 된다.

흔히 풍자를 악의 교정이니, 개선의 의도에서 씌어진 시로 정의한다. 그 때문에 의도적으로 징벌의 대상을 공격하고 헐뜯고, 비아냥하고, 깎아내리고, 비판 고발하는 등의 공격성을 전면에 내세운다. 그러나 이와는 달리 그 배후에는 악의 교정이라는 따뜻한 휴머니티가 작용하게 된다.

전덕기 시인의 풍시조집 『풍시조로 사회정화 운동을』은 사회정화의 기치를 풍시조로 내걸고 외치는 함성 아닌 함성의 메아리가 감동으로 감겨 시대 현실 사회 전반에 울려 퍼지고 있고, 또 이 울림의 메아리는 오늘을 사는 우리들의 벗이 되고 위안이 되어줄 것으로 확신한다. 〈박진환(문학평론가 · 문학박사)〉

The 27th World Poetry Kaya Golden Crown Prize Winner(2013)

The Poetic Anthology Awarded : Be Grateful for Today

수상 시집 : 오늘이 감사하다

*Born at Suncheon, Jeon-Nam, Korea.
*A Director of Korea Headquarters of International Pen Club.
*A Member of Korea Writers' Association of Korea.
*Vice President of Mapo Writers' Association.
*A Director of Recommendation Meeting of Essayist. etc.

Receiving Awards :
*Awarded Main Prize of Heo-nan-sul-heon Literature.
*Awarded a great Prize of Buddhism Literature.
*Awarded a Prize of Essay Literature.
*Awarded a great Heine Literature
*Awarded a great Epi-photo Literature. etc.

Poetical Anthology:
*When the Temple's Ring Says.
*Sonnets for Reeds.
*Longing Mother's Aroma.
*Be Grateful for Today.

*Selected Poems: Walking along the Path of Cherry Blossom.

* 전남 순천 출생
* 국제펜클럽 한국본부 이사
* 한국문인협회 홍보위원
* 마포문인협회 부회장
* 한국수필문학추천작가회 이사 등

■ 수상 경력
* 허난설헌 본상
* 불교문학 대상
* 한국수필 문학상
* 하이네문학상 대상
* 에피포토문학상 대상 외 다수

■ 저서
* 산사의 종이 말할 때
* 갈대연가
* 그리운 어머니 향기
* 오늘이 감사하다

* 선집 : 벚꽃길을 걸으며

Mutual Response with Being and Nature - its Reality

Getting a glance of the poet, Soyeon Jeong Soon-ja's the first poetical anthology, 'Be Grateful for Today', to begin to change the subject of experienced recreation is because her poetic spirit as a source spurting lavas from the poet's inside, flowing through all the poems has its origin from her poetic experience she is keeping.

Generally the poetic aims and the reflection of its images are figured from the created or recreated real life and from the true liveliness streamed out as a poetic truth.

First of all, the motive power of her life, subliming the very experiences make her introspect the self, and make her unsolved problems as poetic subject. Therefore we can find the emotional moving to create the poetic subject through her poetic intuition and her intellectual eyes we can infer the very real life. Such experiences, gained from various things of her life are mixed with her poetic emotion. They are responded to the real things and events she has undergone from her childhood to senescence, and are extracted as several images with a matter of the present time.

If we call this as a direct experience, the diverse phenomena of the unknown world lots of writers or the prophets have written many books, which would be obtained from reading them as an indirect experience, so we have to give attention to the poetic images and the reflection of poetic subject through the indirect experiences in the modern poetry. Therefore her experiences, melted under her inside are due to become 'raison dé être making her write the poems, at the same time, due to make her poetic truth response with nature.

<Kim Song-bae(Poet, Vice President of Korea Writers' Association)>

존재와 자연의 교감 - 그 시적 진실

소연(素蓮) 정순자 시인의 시집 『오늘이 감사하다』를 일별(一瞥)하면서 새롭지도 않은 체험 재생의 화두를 먼저 상기하느냐 하면 이 시집 전체에서 흐르는 의식이 정 시인의 내면에서 용암으로 분출하는 원천이 바로 그가 간직한 소중한 체험에서 발원하고 있기 때문이다.

대체로 정 시인이 탐색하려는 시적 지향점이나 이미지의 투영은 그가 살아온 과거와 현재의 생활 속에서 재생하고 그것들을 재창조한 실생활과 거기에서 창출한 생명성이 시적인 진실로 형상화하고 있다는 점을 간과할 수가 없게 된다.

우선 그의 생활 원동력은 바로 그 체험들을 승화함으로써 자아를 성찰하거나 존재의 오묘한 문제들까지 그의 시상으로 정리하여 시의 본령(本領)으로 정립하고 있어서 현실적인 생활 자체와 자아 경관 등 그 주변에서 생성하는 지적인 혜안을 통한 주제를 창조하려는 정서의 향방을 엿보게 하고 있다. 이런 체험들은 살아오면서 획득된 다양한 삶의 현장이 포괄되어 있다. 이는 태어나서 유년기부터 노년을 거치면서 전개된 삶의 현상이나 겪었던 사건들에서 감응(感應)하거나 감지한 의식의 중심에는 현재라는 시간성과 교감하면서 여러 분류의 이미지를 추출하게 된다.

이것을 직접체험이라 한다면 미지의 세계나 미답(未踏)의 여러 형상들은 선각자나 선지자들이 저술한 많은 지적인 영양소를 독서를 통해 흡수하는 간접체험도 현대시에서 작용하는 이미지나 주제의 투영에 절대적인 역할을 하고 있음을 주목하게 된다.

평소에 심저(心底)에 녹아 흐르게 하는 그것이 존재의 이유이며 자아와 동시에 자연을 교감하는 그의 시적 진실이기 때문이다.〈김송배(시인 · 한국문인협회 부이사장)〉

The 27th World Poetry Kaya Golden Crown Prize Winner(2013)

The Poetic Anthology Awarded : The Mountains Don't Lay the Fault on Clouds
수상 시집 : 산은 구름을 탓하지 않는다

*Born at Suanbo in Chung-ju, Choongbuk, Korea.
*A Member of Korea headquarter in International Pen Club.
*A Director of 25th Public Information of Korea Writers' Association.
*Director for Planning and Management of the World Poetry Institute.
*A Auditor of Seocho Writers' Association.

Receiving Awards :
*Awarded a Prize of the Minister of Education.
*Awarded a great Prize of Tam-Mee Literature.
*Awarded a Prize of Embassy for International Culture Exchange(between Korean and India).
*Awarded a Medal of Nokjoguenjeong(President's)
*Awarded a Prize of Korea Race Literature.

Poetical Anthology :
*A Persimmon Left for Magpie.
*In your Bosom after Becoming a Crane.
*The Mountains Don't Lay the Fault on Clouds. etc.

Publication, etc :
*Bag for Plays, Learning with Playing, 1, 2 vols.
*A Guide of Recreations's Activities.
*Memorial Anthology for Retirement: Fisherman Angling Man.

* 충북 충주 수안보 출생
* 국제펜클럽 한국본부 정회원
* 한국문인협회 25대 홍보위원
* 세계시문학회 기획위원장
* 서초문인협회 감사

■ 수상 경력
* 교육부장관상
* 제8회 탐미문학상 수상
* 국제문화교류상(한국-인도) 대사상 수상
* 녹조근정훈장(대통령상)
* 한국민족문학상

■ 저서
* 까치밥으로 남긴 감 하나
* 학이 되어 그대 품에
* 산은 구름을 탓하지 않는다 외 다수

■ 기타 저서
* 놀며 배우는 놀이주머니 1집, 2집
* 레크레이션 활동의 길잡이
* 정년퇴임 기념문집 「사람을 낚는 어부」

Winner 수상자 : Poet Oh Jin-hwan 오진환(吳鎭煥) 시인

A Lyric Humanism Expressed in Human Nature

The poet, Oh Jin-whan is moving briskly in his daily life after retiring his public duty. So he would like to contribute to the humankind as a holy leader for the citizen's health by laughter curing, church missionary works in native and foreign, various services of social groups, and as a director in the meeting of the World Poetry Institution.

The poet, bearing himself gracefully in modesty to all people, discharge his duty as a moderate master of ceremonies in all audiences. Especially, his unique voice, being sonorous and clear, overwhelmed all audiences. His refined appearance and his active personality gave me as a great intimacy.

In his poem, "Mountains Don't Blame on Clouds" the poet figures the high mountain and the wide sea, the lakes and fields realistically as his own attitude ranging over religion, nature, and literature.

And his suggestive, poetic language together with his generous, charitable sonorous voice, is his own unique characteristic he can express, and is verified as a leading guard of humanism. In his school life, he as a teacher, doesn't covet his promotion, and would like to harmonize between teachers with an attitude of "Being Gentle in Appearance and Sturdy in Spirit" and "A Man of Pure heart and Clean Hands".

Also when hard and difficult problems happened, he would love to throw himself into the matter, so well as calling him as "A Common Giant" displaying in the difficult situation. <The late Kim Joung-woong(Poet, Literary Critic)>

인성에 나타난 서정의 휴머니즘

오진환 시인은 공직에서 정년을 마치고도 일상생활은 매우 분망하다. 웃음 치료로 국민 건강 행복과 교회 전도, 외국 선교와 각종 사회단체 봉사사업, 세계시문학 모임에 중심이 되어 성근스러운 리더로 인류에 공헌하고 있다.

오 시인은 이름 그대로 만인 앞에 정중한 처신을 하여 만인 속으로 들어가 중용으로 다스리는 사회자가 된다. 특히 그의 고유한 음성은 우렁차고 깔끔하여 만인을 압도하는 위용이 스며 있다. 그의 세련된 모습과 호탕한 성격은 필자에게 커다란 친근감으로 다가왔다.

『산은 구름을 탓하지 않는다』에서 오 시인의 시 구현은 종교와 자연과 문학을 섭렵하고 높은 산과 넓은 바다, 호수와 들녘을 리얼리티하게 형상화 한다.

화자의 인품과 같이 너그럽고 인자함이라든가 목소리 우렁찬 발성과 함축성 있는 시어는 오진환 사백만이 갖는 특유의 아미(蛾眉)요, '휴머니즘'의 선구자라는 것을 여실히 증명한다.

그는 교직에서도 승진 상좌를 탐내지 않고, 외유내강(外柔內剛)과 청렴결백(淸廉潔白)한 자세를 갖춘 평교사로 그 학원의 중진이 되어 원만한 조화를 이룬다.

일생을 보통 평범한 사람으로서 생활해 가면서도 불건전한 일이 발생할 때는 중심이 되어 내 일같이 발 벗고 나서서 위대한 힘을 발휘하는 보통 거인(巨人)으로 닉네임이 붙는다. 이러한 인성(人性)에 영원을 불금하리오.

앞으로 시 창작의 열정에 더욱 천착(穿鑿)하기를 기대하는 바다.

〈김정웅(시인 · 문학평론가)〉

The 26th World Poetry Kaya Golden Crown Prize Awarding Ceremony
Commemoration Ceremony For Publication of The 30th Series of World Poetry

- 일시 : 2012년 11월 9일(金) 오후 6시
- 장소 : 대한출판문화회관

第26回 『世界詩 伽倻金冠王冠賞』 施賞式

第30輯(2012) WORLD POETRY(世界詩文學) 出版紀念會

- 主催 : 世界詩文學會 · 乙支出版公社
- 後援 : 한국수력원자력(주)영광원자력본부 · 光州 金病院

Winner 수상자 : Poet Kou Sun-ja 고선자(高善子) 시인

*A Member of Guro Writers' Association.
*A Director of Literary Society of Nature.
*A Director of Public Information of Recitation's Association for Creative Literature of Korea.
*A Member of the World Poetry Institution.
*A Member of Writers' Association of the Literary Movement and Trend.

* 구로문인협회 회원
* 자연문학회 이사
* 한국창작문학낭송협회 홍보위원
* 세계시문학회 회원
* 문예사조문인협회 회원

Sailing to the High Ideal and Intellectual World
- On Kou Sun-ja's Poem, "An Age of Loss"

The poet, Ko Sun-ja's poem, "The Age of Loss" expresses the moderns' afflictions who have developed and enjoyed this civilization. This poem deals with the hard problems between males and females, and of severance of love between member's of their family objectively with her sharp comment, and her cold self-examination.

The poets have charged with the mission recording the age's spirit in objective eyes since old times. We can say that the poet, Ko Sun-ja carried out her duty faithfully only as the poem, who had loved poems and begun to write them since her girlhood.

She appeals to all humans to restore the love between man and man. Thinking over her readiness to write poems, and her resolution to live as a true poet, such a poetic spirit is as beautiful as her external aspect, so we anticipate she will write good poems as a developing poet answering to the above descriptions. Therefore we think she should sail to the high ideal and the intellectual world endless in order to be a courteous and righteous poet.

<A Judging Committee: Choung Song-jun, Kim Kyung-hee>

높은 이상과 지성의 세계를 향해서 항해
- 고선자 시인의 시 '상실시대'

고선자 시인의 「상실시대」는 문명을 지속적으로 발전시켜 향유해온 현대인들의 고뇌가 가득 담긴 내용이다. 세상을 살아가는 남과 여, 또한 가족 구성원들의 사랑의 단절로 인해 파생되는 문제들을 함축시킨 비판과 자성의 목소리가 냉정하리만치 객관화된 작품으로 보여진다.

예로부터 시인의 소명은 주관보다 객관적 시선으로 접근하여 작가가 살았던 시대를 기록하는 사명자로서의 역할을 충실히 수행해야 할 책임감이 맡겨져 있었다. 소녀 시절부터 시를 사랑하며 습작하기 시작했던 고선자 시인은 이 작품 한 편만으로도 사회적 소명의식을 벌써부터 수행하고 있다고 말해줄 수가 있겠다.

사람과 사람 사이에 사랑이 회복되기를 그는 온 인류에게 호소한다. 자나 깨나 펜을 놓지 않는 참 시인으로 살겠다는 각오 또한 대단한 고 시인을 보며 아름다운 미모만큼 여인으로서의 심성과 정의를 신봉하는 여장부다운 결단력 있는 성품으로 보아 앞으로의 詩作들은 급진적 발전을 거듭할 것이라 기대한다. 예의바르고 정의감 있는 시인의 자세를 갖추기 위해 높은 이상과 지성의 세계를 향해 끝없이 항해해야만 하리라. 〈심사 위원 : 이상진 · 신동명 · 김경희〉

W.P 출판기념회 및 「세계시 가야금관왕관상」 시상식(2012)에 국민의례를 하고 있는 참석자들

세계시문학 출판기념회 및 「세계시 가야금관왕관상」 시상식(2012)에 참석한 내빈과 회원들

왕관상을 수상하고 있는
정송전 시인과
시상하고 있는
김정웅 회장과
김계윤 최고자문위원

)시인 Poet, No Jung-ai) 受賞
한출판문화회관

문학 출판기념회 및 제26회 세계시 가야금관 왕관상 시상식
ORATION FOR THE PUBLICATION OF THE WORLD POETRY ANTHOLOGY &

왕관상을 수상하고 있는
진상순 시인과

시상하고 있는
김정웅 회장과
이상진 최고자문위원

문학 출판기념회 및 제26회 세계시 가야금관 왕관상

진상순(陳相順)시인 Poet, Jin Sang-soon) 受賞詩集 : 지구는미령靡寧하시다
(Walking Along the River)

제30집 세계시문학 출판기념회 및 제26회 세계시 가야금관 왕관상 시상식

왕관상을 수상하고 있는
노정애 시인과

시상하고 있는
김정웅 회장과
김일례 이사

THE 26TH AWARDING CEREMONY OF THE
Poet, Choung Song-
Poet, Jin Sang-soon
No Jung-ai) 受
et, Jeong Jin-su)
주최 : 세계시문학

IEMORATION FOR THE PUBLICATION OF THE WORLD POETRY ANTHOLOGY &
DING CEREMONY OF THE KAYA GOLDEN CROWN FOR POETS OF THE
송전(鄭松田)시인 Poet, Choung Song-jun) 受賞詩集 : 내 이렇게 살다가
진상순(陳相順)시인
ng-soon) 受賞詩集 : 학의 장서
(Long Letters of
노정애(盧貞愛)시인
-ai) 受賞詩集 : 지구는
靡寧하시다
정진수(鄭鎭洙)시인
n-su) 受賞
the River)
후 6시 ● 장소 : 대한출판
계시문학회
한수원(주)영광원자력본
月刊 文藝創作

왕관상(王冠賞) : 진상순(陳相順)시인 Poet, Jin Sang-soon) 受賞詩集 : 학의 장서
(Long Letters of A Crane)
왕관상(王冠賞) : 노정애(盧貞愛)시
No Jung-a
詩集 : 지구는미령靡寧하시다
신인상(新人賞) : 정진수(鄭鎭洙)시
Jeong J
일시 : 2012. 11. 9(金) 오후 6시 ● 장소 : 대한
● 주최 :
을지출판공
수원(주
본부

문학상을 수상하고 있는
정진수 시인과

시상하고 있는
김정웅 회장과
윤해규 상임자문위원

(Long Letters of A Crane)
하시다
n Is Indisposed)
the River)
: 한수원(주)영
본부
月刊 文藝創

: 진상순(陳相
: 노정애(盧貞
: 정진수(鄭鎭
오후 6시 ● 장소 :

문학 출판기념회 및 제26회 세계시 가야금관 왕관상 시상식
ORATION FOR THE PUBLICATION OF THE WORLD POETRY ANTHOLOGY &
G CEREMONY OF THE KAYA GOLDEN CROWN FOR POETS OF THE WORLD POETRY
(鄭松田)시인 Poet, Choung Song-jun) 受賞詩集 : 내 이렇게 살다가 (Living As Yearning)
(陳相順)시인 受賞詩集 : 학의 장서
(盧貞愛)시인 受賞詩集
(鄭鎭洙)시인 g Jin-su)
● 장소 : 대한출판

문학 출판기념회 및 제26회 세계시 가야금관 왕관상 시상식
ORATION FOR THE PUBLICATION OF THE WORLD POETRY ANTHOLOGY &
G CEREMONY OF THE KAYA GOLDEN CROWN FOR POETS OF THE WORLD POETRY
선(鄭松田)시인 Poet Song-jun) 受賞詩集 살다가 (Living As Yearning)
순(陳相順)시인 soon) 受賞詩集 (Long Letters of
애(盧貞愛)시인 ai) 受賞詩集 : 하시다
수(鄭鎭洙)시인 n-su) 受賞詩 : the River)
● 장소 : 대한출판문화회관 세계시문학회 · 을지출판공 한수원(주)영광원자력 金病院 · 月刊 文藝創作

The Earth Is

왕관상(王冠賞) : 정송전(鄭松田)시인 Poet, Choung Song-jun) 受賞
왕관상(王冠賞) : 진상순(陳相順)시인 Poet, Jin Sang-soon) 受賞詩
노정애(盧貞愛)시인 Poet,
受賞詩集 :
세계시문학회 · 을지출

정송전(鄭松田)시인 Poet, Choung Song-jun) 受賞詩集
진상순(陳相順)시인 Poet, Jin Sang-soon) 受賞詩集 : 학의
노정애(盧貞愛)시인 Poet, No Jung-ai) 受賞詩集
정진수(鄭鎭洙)시인 Poet, Jeong Jin-su)
오후 6시
장소 :

THE 30TH COMMEMORATION FOR THE PUBLICATION OF
THE 26TH AWARDING CEREMONY OF THE KAYA GOLDEN
왕관상(王冠賞) : 정송전(鄭松田)시인 Poet, Choung Song-jun) 受賞
왕관상(王冠賞) : 진상순(陳相順)시인 Poet, Jin Sang-soon) 受賞詩集
노정애(盧貞愛)시인
정진수(鄭鎭洙)시인
오후 6시
주최 :

세계시문학회
회원들의 시낭송

왕관상(王冠賞)
시인 Poet
왕관상(王冠
시인 Poet
왕관상(王冠
시인 Poet
신인상(新
시인 Poet
일시 : 2012. 11. 9(金)
대한출판문화회관

Jung-ai) 受賞詩集 :
ng Jin-
주최 : 세계
을지출판

왕관상(王冠賞) : 진상순(陳相
노정애(盧貞愛
진수(鄭鎭洙
6시 · 장소 :

oet, Jeong Jin-su) 受賞
화회관
문학회 · 을

The 31st World Poetry Symposium

The World Poetry Institute held the 31st World Poetry Symposium in Kochang, Junbuk, Korea from July, 17-18, 2013. It was progressed by the master of ceremonies, the poet, Choung Song-jun: They were the 1st thematic speech: <John Donne and his Metaphysical Poetry> by the Poet, Won Eung-soon, and 2nd speech: <Literature for Recitation and Vocalization> by the poet, Kim Joung-woong, and after the two poet's speeches, we had the heated controversy and lastly, recitation of W.P. Memebers poems, and recreation for all. Therefore this symposium was a great success.

第31次 世界詩文學 심포지엄

본회는 금년 7월 17일~18일까지 W. P 제31차 세계시문학 심포지엄을 전북 고창에서 개최했다. 좌장이신 정송전 시인의 사회로 발표자 원응순 시인은 〈존 던과 형이상학 시〉, 김정웅 시인은 〈낭송문학과 발성법〉에 대한 주제 발표가 있은 후 진지한 토론을 가졌으며, 끝으로 시낭송 및 레크리에이션으로 성황리에 마쳤다.

2013 Gochang Summer Symposium of the World Poetry & Reading Poems
Subject : John Donne and Metaphysical ---Won Eung-soon , Ph.D. / Voclization for Peading Poems---Kim Joung-woong,Ph.D
祝
2013 세계시문학 여름 심포지움과 시낭송
주제 :1.「형이상학시의 존던」 원응순(시인 영문학교수) 2.「낭송문학과 발성법」 김정웅(시인 W.P회장)
일시 : 2013년 7월17~18일(1박2일) 장소 : 아산면 선운사로 우체국수련원 주최 : 세계 시문학회 후원 : 고창군, 미래과학창조부,고창우체국
祝

세계시문학심포지엄

미당 시 문학관
Poet Midang Memorial Hall
CCTV

World Poetry

世界詩文學 세계시문학

Vol.31/2013

EDITOR : CHOUNG SONG-JUN
TRANSLATOR : WON EUNG-SOON

그림 : 조기현(시인·화가)

EulJi Publishing Company
을지출판공사
Republic Of Korea

WORLD POETRY 世界詩文學 세계시문학
Vol.31 / 2013
(price; $20)

EDITOR : Choung Song-jun

TRANSLATOR : Won Eung-soon

Published by : Kim Hyo-yeol / 金 孝 洌
EulJi Publishing Company 乙支出版公社
〈등록번호 제 2-741호 1985. 2. 14 등록〉
394-81, Seogyo-dong, Mapo-gu, Seoul, 121-840, Korea
TEL (02) 334-4050 FAX (02) 334-4010
e-mail : ejp4050@hanmail.net

Pubilshed on November 29, 2013. Printed on November 25, 2013

COPYRIGHT : President Choung Song-jun

THE WORLD POETRY INSTITUTE
394-81, Seogyo-dong, Mapo-gu, Seoul, 121-840, Korea
Tel. 82-2-334-4050 Mobile 82-19-234-8416, 82-10-8747-4050

CONTENTS

COLOMBIA

ENGLAND

KOREA

World Poetry Translators

Names of Translators	Names of Translators
ADA AHARONI	HELLEN WONL PATTERSON
AILA O.COMES	HUCH MCKNLEY
ALAIN PIOTE CLAUDIA FLURY	IH MING-UH
AMY WAGNER	INGE DREYER
AN CHO-GEUN	JAIME GARCIA GARCIA
ANDRÉA DE PAULA SANTOS	JANE MAISKAYA
ANDRE BOUCHIER	JEANNE MAILLET
ANGELA PAIVA DE LUCIO	JEONG WI-JIN
ANTONIO AUGUSTO ULBUM	JIN CHEN-HUI
A.PAULA SANTOS	JN ARA DEADRLNS
A.S.DAWSON	JIN XUE-SHONG
A.SIMON DE SOUZA	JOANNE VARRICCHIO
BLACK EARL	JOHN ROBERTS
BETTINA HERR	JO MAN-HO
CARLA KRAUS	JO YUN-KYU
CHANG SOO-CHEOL	KANG SHIN-IL
CHANG SOON-BOK	KANG TONG-WON
CINDY CHILDO	KAPONE JULIE
CHOI SEI-KYUN	KAREN ALKALAY-GUT
CHONG YUN-BOM	KIM BYUNG-RIN
DAVID MACANN	KIM DONG-SOO
DENISE LEVERTOV	KIM DONG SUNG
DOLORES PEREDA	KIM JAI-HIUN
DOROTHEA	KIM IK-JE
ESTHER CAMERON	KIM IM-SUK
EVA SHALTIEL	KIM IN KYUNG
EVI PAPADIMA THEODORAKIS	KIM JOO-SENG
GE	KIM KWANG-BAE
FERNANDO ALONSO BARAHONA	KIM MAN-GON
G.PALUMBO	KIM MIN-SEONG
GUENI G.Z.AIMOF	KIM SANG-HWAN
HADASSAH HASKELE	KIM SENG-HUI
HAN IN-SOON	KIM YOUN-JAE
HAN SONG-SUN	KIM YOUNG-NAM
HANS-DIETER LUCKE	KIM YOUNG-SAM

Names of Translators	Names of Translators
KIM YUHN-BOK	ROBERTO MORAES PEREIRH
KOH CHANG-SOO	RO CHANG-SHIK
KIM YONG-SUN	RURIKO SUZUKI
KIM YUHN-BOK	RUTH PELDMAN
LEE BO-HEA	SEIJI HINO
LEE HEE-SEON	SHIM SANG-WOOK
LEE HE-YOUNG	SHIN MYONG-HO
LEE JONG-HWAN	SHIN TONG-CHOON
LEE JOON-YOUNG	SHIRA TWERSKY-CASSEL
LEE JUNG-KEE	SHULAMITS NARDI
LEE TAI-DONG	SONG IN-SOB
LEE YOUNG-GUL	SON SUCK-RIN
LI JAI-SIK	SON Y.S.
LI JONG WHAN	STEPHEN BADZIK
LIM HO-SOON	TAKEKAZY HISADA
LIM HYE-RYEON	SYM M.H.
LIVIA PAULINI	TAKESHI ISHIARA
LUIS A.SANCHEZ	TERESINKA PEREIRA
LUIS MUNIZ	TINA SALLEE
MAIA CIRCE	TUIS MUNIZ
MENTIRAS	VELTA SNIKERE
MIRABEL	VICKIE DIMITRIADON
MOHAMED SELMI	VICTOR OURIN
MOON SUL-CHANG	WAN HUA GOH CHAPOUTHER
NILSA Y.GARZA	WERMER MANHEIM
NOBUKO NAKAMURA	XIMENA CORTES
O.C.KIM PH.D	YEO HONG-SANG
OH CHEOL	YU JEONG-SUK
PARK JOOON-TAE	YOO YEONG
PARK SOON-WON	YOON CHONG-HIOK
PARK TAE-JIN	YOON GANG-WON
PARK YONG-JIN	YU IN-HO
PARK YOUNG-SU	ZEV DAVIS
RENE STREIFF	PARK, MEEN-HEUM
RIE LEIGH-LOOHUIZEN	KIM KWANG-OUP
ROBERT LEARNELY	WON EUNG-SOON

Winners of KAYA Golden Crown World Poets Award

Year	Country	Name of Winners
1986	KOREA	KIM IL-RO
1987	KOREA	LEE HAN-HO
	U.S.A.	ROSEMARY C.WILKINSON
1988	U.S.A.	VICTORY OURINE
	KOREA	MOON DEOK-SOO
	C. I. S.(RUSSIA)	DOLMA TOVSKY EUGINE
	ESPANA	TOMAS BEVIA ARANDA
	INDIA	D.K.JOY
1989	KOREA	SHIN DONG-JIP
	U.S.A.	ELLIS OVESEN
	YUGO(Sarajevo)	DR. AJSA ZAHIROVIC
	KOREA	JEONG KI-SEOK
1990	U.S.A.	DR. MARY J. BANERS
	KOREA	DR. KIM DONG-NI
	KOREA	DR. YUN JONG-HYOK
1991	JAPAN	UEMOTO MASAO
	KOREA	LIM JI-HYUN
	AUSTRALIA	JOY BEAUDETTE CRIPS
	KOREA	LIM HEON-DO
1992	KOREA	BAEK HAN-YI
	BRAZIL	ANGELA MARIA ROCHA BIASE
	KOREA	YANG SANG-WOOK
	CHINA P.R.	CHEN-HUI JIN
1993	KOREA	KIM JI-HYANG
	ISRAEL	ADA AHARONI
	JAPAN	JUNKO HAMAE
	KOREA	DR. KIM JOUNG-WOONG
	CHINA P.R.	Prof. LU JIN

Year	Country	Name of Winners
1994	KOREA	CHOI YUN-YOUNG
1995	KOREA	LEE CHANG-HWAN
1996	KOREA	SON KI-SUB
1997	KOREA	KIM MIN-SEONG
1998	KOREA	KIM NAM-WOONG
	KOREA	KIM CHUI-KYONG
1999	KOREA	LEE JAE-HYUN
	KOREA	JUNG SOON-YOUNG
	KOREA	PARK KEUN-HOO
2000	KOREA	JIN EUL-JU
	CHINA	GE NAI FU
2001	KOREA	LEE KI-BAN
2002	JAPAN	JUN UENO
2003	KOREA	KIM CHANG-JIK
	KOREA	KIM JI-WON
2004	JAPAN	NATIKO WATANABE
	KOREA	CHUNG OK-IN
2005	KOREA	SEO JEONG-NAM
	KOREA	LEE JI-YOUNG
	KOREA	JUNG U-HA
2006	KOREA	OH MIN-PHIL
	KOREA	KIM SUNG-YOUL
	KOREA	LEE JONG-IL
2007	KOREA	SHIN SOON-AE
	KOREA	CHO KI-HYUN
2008	KOREA	CHOI SEUNG-BEOM
	KOREA	KANG HAE-KUN

Year	Country	Name of Winners
2009	KOREA	SHIN DONG-MYEUNG
	KOREA	KIM JONG-WON
2010	KOREA	PARK MOON-JAE
	KOREA	LIM WON-SIK
	KOREA	EUN YO-SUK
2011	KOREA	KIM KYE-YOON
	KOREA	KIM IL-RYE
2012	KOREA	CHOUNG SONG-JUN
	KOREA	JIN SANG-SOON
	KOREA	NO JUNG-AI
2013	KOREA	JUN DUK-KI
	KOREA	JUNG SUN-JA
	KOREA	OH JIN-HWAN

An Address

For the Prosperity of the Open World Poetry

The World Poetry Research was organized in Nov. 1982 (by the poet, Kim Young-sam, 1st President), and it was adorned with its 31 year history until the 2nd president, the late Kim Joung-woong (may his soul rest in peace).

I am sure that the World Poetry has provided a great momentum for exchange of the world poetic literature and the cultural promotion of the world poets through our 31 volumes of anthologies, and has created a sphere of poetry, expressing our poems of 8 hundreds of poets from 60 countries over the world through them.

Especially, I am proud, the World Poetry Kaya Gold Crown Prize(awarded 27th prize in total, on 18 foreign poets and on 51 native poets) won't be too much to say it at the highest estimate on a great achievement carried out by only our World Poetry, and in addition to this, which was sent as 4000 volumes for the collection of library to the famous library over the world.

Now as the 3rd President of the World Poetry, I feel a heavy responsibility taking over the President.

Earnestly I entreat you all our World Poetry Members to take care of our World Poetry's prosperity being well matched to the open future age, and I wish you to have good health and literary enlightenment.

Thank you all.

President Choung Song-jun

열린 시문학회의 융성을 위하여

세계시문학회는 1982년 11월 창립하여(초대 회장 김영삼 시인) 2대 회장 김정웅 시인에 이르기까지(2013. 9. 15) 31년의 연륜을 쌓아 왔습니다.

그동안, 제31집에 이르는 세계시문학 작품집 발간을 통해 세계 시인들의 시문학 교류와 문화 창달의 크나큰 계기를 마련하였으며, 세계 60여 개국 800여 현역시인들과의 작품 교류로 문자 그대로 시의 한바탕을 이루었다고 해서 지나친 말이 아닙니다.

특히, 1986년부터 시작한 세계시가야금관왕관상(총 27회 시상에 18명의 외국시인을 비롯 총 69명 시상)은 세계시문학회만이 이루어 낼 수 있었던 빛나는 업적으로 평가받아 마땅하다는 생각입니다.

현재 4,000여 권의 World Poetry가 세계 유수한 대학도서관의 장서가 된 업적 또한 빠뜨릴 수 없는 것입니다.

이에, 그 뒷자리를 이어받는 것 또한 막중한 것이어서 어깨가 무거울 수밖에 없습니다.

열린 시대에 걸맞게 열린 세계시문학회의 융성을 위하여 회원 여러분의 배전의 편달을 당부하는 바이며, 건승과 문운이 함께 하시길 빕니다.

세계시문학회 회장 鄭 松 田

Member of World Poetry Institute (2013)

Nation	Name	Domicile	Position
Korea	Lee Ki-ban	11-301, Korong Apt, 1-ga, Pyeonghwa-dong, Wansan-gu, Jeonju-city, Jeon-buk, 560-779, Korea	Senior Advisor
Korea	Choi Seung-beom	361-8, Jinbuk-dong, Deokjin-gu, Jeonju-si, Jeonbuk, Korea	Senior Advisor
Korea	Lee Sang-jin	Director at the legal office, 458-88, Mangwon-dong, Mapo-gu, Seoul, Korea	Supreme Advisory Committee
Korea	Choung Song-jun	201-201, Paradise Apt. #123-1 Songjeongdong, Gwangju City, Geonggido, Korea.	President
Korea	Ahn Byung-don	145-3,Docheongmyeon, Buangun, Jeon-Buk, Korea.	
Korea	Ahn Jae-woon	102, Ga-dong, Geonyang Apt, 681-45, eupnae-ri, gochang-eup, gochang-gun, jeonbuk	
Korea	Ahn Jun-hee	609, mujigae Apt 3dong, seocho-dong, seocho-gu, Seoul city Korea	
Korea	Ahn In-sil	1306-1005, Jugong Apt, Chelsan-dong, Gwang myeong-si, Gyeonggi-do, 423-030, Korea	
Korea	Bae Myoung-sik	1th, 278-97, Sadang4-dong, Dongjak-gu, Seoul, 156-821, Korea	
Korea	Bae Young-suk	102-302, Dongseong Apt, Yeonhyang-dong Suncheon-city, Jeon-nam, 540-761, Korea	
Korea	Baek Bong-ki	103, 116dong, Hyundae apt, ajung-ri, Inhu1-dong Deokjin-gu, Jeonju-city, Jeon-buk, 561-781, Korea	
Korea	Baek Deok-sun		
Korea	Baek Han-yi	837-4, Hwagok4-dong, Gangseo-gu, Seoul, 157-014, Korea	
Korea	Bang Jung-sun	360, jaryong-ri, Sangha-myeon, Gochang-gun, Jeonbuk, 585-910, Korea	
Korea	Bark Il-so	603, 101 dong, wolgye 2 dong, nowon-gu, Seoul, Korea	Director
Korea	Chae Eun-sun Olive(미국 이름)	2012 Devonshire Dr Fort Collins, co 80526-2301 U.S.A	
Korea	Cho Keum-ja	191-15, Eupnae-ri, Gochang-eup, Gochang-gun, Jeon-buk, 585-807, Korea	
Korea	Cho Ki-hyun	102, 5-dong, Hanjung villa, Chun-chun-ri, Maesong-myeon, Whasong city, Gyeong-gi province	

Nation	Name	Domicile	Position
Korea	Choi Byeong-ryun	204-703, Jugong Apt. Soosungdong, Jeongeup City, Jeon-Buk, Korea.	
Korea	Choi Hye-sook	305-804, Humansia Apt. Sangdong, Jeoneup City, Jeon-Buk, Korea.	
Korea	Choi Jung-sook	204-109, Myungcheon-Jugong Apt., Myungcheondong, Boryung City, Chung-Nam, Korea.	Director of Central Division
Korea	Choi Jae-eon	201-1, Eupnae-ri, Gochang-eup, Gochang-gun, Jeon-buk, Korea	
Korea	Choi Kil-soon	19tong 7ban, #463-12, Myunmok 3-dong, Jungryang-gu, Seoul, Korea.	
Korea	Choi Moo-ja	Seohae Grangble Apt. 106-503, Geoman-dong, Seo-gu, Incheon City.	
Korea	Choi Sun-ae	489-1 Jekok-dong Suncheon-City Jeonnam 540-110 Korea	Director
Korea	Choi Yong-kwang	1701, Shinhyundae APT, Shiheung 5dong, Geumcheongu, Seoul	
Korea	Choi Yun-seon		
Korea	Eun Hee-tae	17-5, Aenggok-gil, Gobu-myeon, Jeongeup-city, Jeon-buk, Korea.	
Korea	Eun Yo-suk	1638-5, Sinlim Bon-Dong, Gwanak-gu, Seoul,151-029, Korea	Vice President
Korea	Gwon O-un	2201-407, Moonlight Village, Whajungdong, Deokyanggu, Goyang City, Gyeonggido, Korea.	
Korea	Han Gwi-nam	2-61 Gyedong, Jongnogu, Seoul, Korea.	
Korea	Hong Chon-an	118-2106, Donga Chongsol Apt, Chang4-dong, Dobong-gu, Seoul,132-791, Korea	
Korea	Hong Chun-pyo	Guro 6dong Namyang Building 401,136-40,Guro-gu	
Korea	Hong Seong-su	313-405, Myungcheon-Jugong 4th Apt., Myungcheondong, Boryung, Chung-Nam.	
Korea	Hong Kwang-seon	108-1302, Kanseok Pungrim Apt. A-dong, Kanseok-dong, 935, Namdong-gu, Incheon-city, Korea	
Korea	Hong Yang-ja	45-83, Muak-dong, Jongno-gu, Seoul, 110-813, Korea	
Korea	Hong Yun-pyeo	2238-1, Namsan-ri, Dang-jin-eup, Dangjin-gun, Chung-nam, 343-802, Korea	

Nation	Name	Domicile	Position
Korea	Hwang Seong-ee	307-907, Silver Light Apt. Sangge 1-dong, Nowongu, Seoul, Korea.	
Korea	Hwang Song-hae	101-502, Hangang Apt, Hyoja-dong, Wansan-gu, Jeonju-si, 560-891, Korea	
Korea	Jang Eun-hae	376-33, Hungnung 3rd-dong, Seongbukgu, Seoul, Korea.	
Korea	Jang Hyun-kyung	40-3, Joongkog 2nd Dong, Gwangjingu, Seoul, Korea.	
Korea	Jang Seong-yeon	102-504, Ujangsan Lotte Apt, 1148, Hwagok6-dong, Gangseo-gu, Seoul, 157-916, Korea	
Korea	Jeon Yu-yeong	102-206 Woosungsinsung Apt., Pyungwha 2nd-Dong, Wansangu, Jeon-Buk.	
Korea	Jeong Ji-ahn	Rm 207, 103-dong Hyundai Green Apt., Sigok-ri Dangjin-up Dangjin-gun Chung nam, 343- 753, Korea	
Korea	Jeong Ji-won		Director
Korea	Jeong Jin-su	4384, Singil 4-dong, Samsung Layan Apt. 106-301, Youngdeungpogu, Seoul, Korea	Vice Secretary General
Korea	Jeong Mi-na	Hand Phone: 010-4782-5881	
Korea	Jeong Won-hwan	Seongnam-ri, Daesan-myeon, Gochang-gun, jeon-buk, 585-860, Korea	
Korea	Jeong Yeong-hwan	73-10, Gyochon-ri, Gochang-eup, Gochang-gu, Jeon-buk, 585-800, Korea	
Korea	Jin Myong-sook	805-102, Jugong Apt., Ha-An 2nd-dong, Gwang-myung City, Geonggido Korea.	
Korea	Jin Sang-soon	707, 101dong, Hyundae Apt, 315-1, Sinpung-dong, Kimje-city, Jeon-buk, 570-804, Korea	Director
Korea	Jo Dal-ho	1093-23, Pyong-ri 3 dong, Seogu, Daegu megalopolis city, Korea.	
Korea	Jo Hwa-hun	1301, Myeongji carat Apt, 535-5, Anyang6-dong, Manan-gu, Anyang-si, Korea	
Korea	Jun Duk-ki	147, Dongsomundong 4ga, Seongbukgu, Seoul, Korea.	Supreme Advisory Committee
Korea	Jung Sun-ja	247-162, Seokyodong, Mapogu, Seoul, Korea.	Director
Korea	Jung Ok-im	5-305, Saneopin Apt., Gocheokdong, Gurogu, Seoul, Korea.	

Nation	Name	Domicile	Position
Korea	Jung U-ha	106, 105dong, Daewoo Apt, Yeonhyang-dong, Suncheon-city, Jeon-nam, 540-762, Korea	
Korea	Kang Chang-won	1205, Woojueunha Apt., 511-3, Sinjinri, Gwang choneup, Hongseonggun, Chung Nam, Korea.	
Korea	Kang Hae-kun	102-108, Kyunyoung apt, 72-3, Munjeong-dong, Songpa-gu, Seoul, 138-200, Korea	
Korea	Kang Jeong-ae	103, 203dong, Dongseong Apt, 35, Bundang-dong, Bundand-gu, Seonam-city, Gyeonggi-do, 463-747, Korea	
Korea	Kang Sang-ku	932-2, Duam 3rd-dong, Bukgu, Gwangju Metropolitan City, Korea	
Korea	Kang Young-duk	1-202, Daehan apt., 381-18, Hwagok7-dong, Gangseo-gu, Seoul, 157-885. Korea	
Korea	Kim A-lang	102-806, Chunggu Apt, shinbanpo, jamwondong, seochogu, Seoul, Korea	
Korea	Kim Ae-yeong	1109, 101dong, Sindonga Tower, Banyeo1-dong, Haeundae-gu, Busan-city, 612-061, Korea	
Korea	Kim Baek-kyeong		Director
Korea	Kim Bok-nam	101-1205, Dongguk Apt, 1034-1, Jinbuk2-dong, Deogjin-gu, Jeonju-si, Jeon-buk, 561-782, Korea	Director of Management
Korea	Kim Chong-ki	621, Sanghadong, Giheunggu, Yongin City, Suwon-dongmaeul Ssangyong Apt. 303-1701, Geonggido, Korea.	
Korea	Kim Don-young	311-13, Bulkwangdong, Metrotower 2206, Eunpyunggu, Seoul Korea.	Head of News Gathering
Korea	Kim Eui-sik	328-7, Gildong 2nd-dong, Gangdonggu, Hanma eum-Jutaek 401, Seoul, Korea.	Director of Traditional Culture Research Institute
Korea	Kim Gui-rye	1802, 301dong, 3th, Nueung Apt, Bongseon-dong, Nam-gu, Gwangju-city, 503-760, Korea	Director of Inquiry Commission
Korea	Kim Hak-jin	346, Yonggye-dong, Jeongeup-si, Jeon-buk, 580-230, Korea	
Korea	Kim Hye-sook	#10 1Gil Nosong Square, Wansan-Gu, Jeonju City Korea	Director
Korea	Kim Hyo-yeol	394-81, Seogyo-dong, Mapo-gu, Seoul 121-840, Korea	Secretary General
Korea	Kim Hyung-chol	351, Bonghwang-ri, Dongjin-Myeon, Buan-gun, Jeon-Buk, Korea	
Korea	Kim IL-rye	E-mail : kimilrye@hotmail.com	Director

Nation	Name	Domicile	Position
Korea	Kim Jae-kyun	1357-2, Yongbongdong, I-House 2nd Floor, Korea.	
Korea	Kim Ji-won	Gyeonseong grotto, San 3 Songneung 1-ri, Jinkeon-eup, Namyangju-city, Gyeonggi-do, 472-830, Korea	
Korea	Kim Ji-yeol	160, Ilsim-ri, Hwasun-eup, Hwasun-gun, Jeon-nam, 519-809, Korea	
Korea	Kim Jin-soo	401, Chungdam Park View, 61-11, Chungdam-dong, Gannamgu, Seoul.	
Korea	Kim Jong-hee	337-36 Seokyodong, Mapogu, Seoul, Korea	
Korea	Kim Kwang-Ja	118-1805, kyongnam sunkyong Apt., 1448, haiwundaigu, Busan city, Korea	
Korea	Kim Kye-yoon	Kim Hospital, 161-2, Daemin-dong, Dong-gu, Gwangju-city, 501-030, Korea	Supreme Advisory Committee
Korea	Kim Kyeong-soon	Sinsungmisogium@ 302-501, Samsan-2-dong, Bupyeong-Gu, Inchon City, Korea	Director of Reciting & Illustrated Poems
Korea	Kim Kyung-hee	1269, Guro-Bondong, Gurogu, Jungang Apt., 10-1901, Seoul.	Chief Editor
Korea	Kim Mi-kyoung	Boramaedong, Gwanakgu, Boramae Samsung Apt. 101-1502, Seoul, Korea.	Vice Secretary General
Korea	Kim Min-joong	442-2, Pyeongsa-ri, Sanoe-myeon, Jeongeup-city, Jeon-buk, 580-950, Korea	
Korea	Kim Nam-Woung	2430, 106dong, Dodeok Park Town, 625, Chulsan 4dong, Gwangmyeong city, Kyongki-do	
Korea	Kim Sang-kyung	361-1 Hwagok 1-dong, Kangseo-gu, Hwagok Daelim Apt. 5-1504, Seoul	
Korea	Kim Sang-hyun	608-202, Hanguk Apt, 727-2, Sin-gok-dong, Uijeongbu-si, Gyeonggi-do, 480-787, Korea	
Korea	Kim Sang-soo	581-13, samcheondong-1ga, wansan-gu, Jeonju-si, Jeonbuk	
Korea	Kim Seok-ki	40-2, Jungangdong, Gwachun City, Geonggido, Seoul.	
Korea	Kim Seon-chul	489, Gesanmyun, Asanri, Kochanggun, Jeon-Buk, Korea.	
Korea	Kim Shin-jeong	567-3(1st floor), Hannamdong, Yongsangu, Seoul, Korea.	
Korea	Kim So-yeop	261, Chungsoodong ,Chunan City, Chung-Nam, Sunkyung Apt. 112-601.	

Nation	Name	Domicile	Position
Korea	Kim Song-bae	112-44, naresilgil 40-1, yeonhee 1-dong, seodaemun-gu, Seou,l Korea	
Korea	Kim Sun	301 Ho, 105 Dong, Joyparkvill, 139-6, NamSan-ri, PaengSeong-eub, PyeongTaek-Si, Gyeonggi-do, 451-803, Korea.	Director
Korea	Kim Sung-youl	room 611-1103, dongmoon good morning Apt, Supsokkil maul, dongpe-ri 1687, kyoha-eup, paju si, Gyeonggi-do	
Korea	Kim Whoa-ja	487, Sajeong-dong, Joong-gu, Woonamstawon 101-801, Daejeon City.	Director
Korea	Kim Woon-jung	529-159 Bupyungdong, Bupyunggu, Palbangsan, Incheon City, Korea.	Director
Korea	Kim Young-mi	9-405, Boram Apt, Bondong, Gurogu, Seoul, Korea.	Director
Korea	Kim Young-mi	422-1 Sam-Lee, Gonjiam-Eup, Hyun-yeunrip B-dong, #103, Kwangju City, Kyunggi-do, Korea	Director
Korea	Ko Bang-kyu	463, Okjeri, Gochanggun, Jeon-Buk, Korea.	
Korea	Ko Seon-ok	102-1704, Hyundae Apt. Sukyori, Gochangeup, Gochang gun, Jeon-Buk, Korea.	
Korea	Koo Soon-ja	384-28, Mangwondong, Mapogu, Seoul, Korea.	
Korea	Koo Ja-cheol		
Korea	Kuk Mi-na	Hand Phone: 010-6799-3949. E-mail: kuk8989@naver.com	
Korea	Kwak Byung-soo	1704-102dong, Deokhyeon Apt, 808, Gyomun2-dong, Guri-city, Geonggi-do, Korea.	
Korea	Lee Byeong-chang	462, Shindeok-ri, Shindeok-myeon, Limsil-gun, Jeon-buk, Korea	
Korea	Lee Byung-Seok	#15, 110Gil, Gaepo-dong, Gangnam-Gu, Woosung 7th @ 115-803, Seoul, Korea.	Director
Korea	Lee Chang-hwan	176-3, Seobu-dong Yeongyang-Eup Youngyang-gun Kyeongbuk 764-800 Korea	
Korea	Lee Chung-hee		
Korea	Lee Deok-Sang	Geumgan Venturetel #1704, 1108 Bisandong, Dongangu,Anyangsi,Gyeonggido	
Korea	Lee Eun-hyeop	6-4, Daejodong, Eunpyeonggu, Seoul, Korea.	

Nation	Name	Domicile	Position
Korea	Lee Ji-soo	101-1205, Haeju Apt, 55, Sangha-ri, Hongnong-eup, Yeong-gwang-gun, Jeon-nam, 513-884, Korea	
Korea	Lee Ji-young	Rm 1002, 311-Dong Dongah Apt Dream Town, Pyungchon-dong, Dongan-gu, Anyang-City Gyeonggi-do, Korea	
Korea	Lee Kyeong-hwa		
Korea	Lee Jong-il	205, Anam apt. 9, Macheon2-dong, Songpa-gu, Seoul, 138-120, Korea	
Korea	Lee Jun-sil	691, Sangyedong, Nowongu, Jugong Apt. 718-1302, seoul Korea.	
Korea	Lee Kang	502, na-dong, Daemyeong Apt, Seoseohak-dong, Wansan-gu, Jeonju-city, Jeon-buk, 560-130, Korea	
Korea	Lee Kyu-sae	514-801, Jugong Apt, 702, Haan1-dong, Gwang myeong-si, Gyeonggi-do, Korea	
Korea	Lee Moon-ho	410, 101dong, Hyundai Apt, 785-1, Daerim3-dong, Yeongdeungpo-gu, seoul, 150-073, Korea	
Korea	Lee Sang-mok	954, 2nd Floor, Dogok-dong, Seoul, Korea.	
Korea	Lee Sin-kang	108-4, dunchon 2dong, gangdong-gu, Seoul, Korea	
Korea	Lee Su-jung	14 floor- 1, 102dong, Hyundai Apt 203-6, Deokgei-dong, yangju city, Geongkido	
Korea	Lim In-chol	707-1003, Mokryun Woosung Apt., Beomgyedong, Dongangu, Anyang City, Geonggido, Korea.	Director
Korea	Lim Won-sik	933-4, Wolsan 4-dong, Namgu, Gwangju Metropolitan city, Korea.	
Korea	Min Byung-hyu	101-1005, Namhae Onetteu vill, 508, Unrim-dong, Dong-gu, Gwangju-si, 501-200, Korea	
Korea	Min Suk-young	Apt 401, 490-5, Wolpi-dong, Sangrok-gu, Ansan-city, Gyeonggi-do, 425-070, Korea	
Korea	Nam Byung-geun	930, Baeseokdong, Cheonan City, Brownstone Apt. 108-301, Chung-Nam, Korea.	
Korea	Namgung Yeon-ok	722-2, Gongheung the 3rd-ri, Yangpyung eup, Yangpyungun, Geonggido, Korea.	
Korea	No Jung-ai	142-8, Daehyun-dong, Seodaemon-gu, Seoul, 120-170, Korea	
Korea	Oh Hui-chang	202, 1402dong, Mokdong Apt, 329, Sinjeong6-dong, Yangcheon-gu, Seoul, 158-076, Korea	

Nation	Name	Domicile	Position
Korea	Oh Jin-hwan	2-202, Kyeong-nam Apt, 1-8 Banpo-dong, Seocho-gu, Seoul, 137-765, Korea	Director of Planning
Korea	Oh Keum-ja	31-3, Seongju 5-ri, Seongjumyeon, Boryung City, Chung-Nam.	
Korea	Oh Min-phil	45-1, Hakseong-dong, Jung-gu, Ulsan-city, 681-822, Korea	
Korea	Park Eun-seok	101 Daseong Villa, #173-6, Sonpa 2nd-dong, Songpagu, Seoul, Korea.	
Korea	Pak Ky-tae	102, Na-dong, Gwangjin Apt, 213-2, Hyojadong1-ga, Wansan-Gu, Jeonju-si, Jeon-buk, Korea	
Korea	Park In-ae	Reside in Dallas City, Texas, US	
Korea	Park Keun-hoo	449-4, Sang-dong , Jeongeup-city, Jeon-buk,. 580-801, Korea	
Korea	Park Moon-jae	417-1 Songbaek Village, Mokwangri, Yangseo myun, Yangpyunggun , Gyeonggido, Korea.	
Korea	Park Youn-ki	322-90 Chosan-ri, Habuk-myun, Yangsan City, Kyung-nam, Korea	Director
Korea	Park Sam-suk	1411, 103dong, Jungheung Apt, Yongbong-dong, Buk-gu, Gwangju-si, 500-070, Korea	
Korea	Seo Jeong-il	31-10 dongilro 104, 212 changamdong, euijeongbu city, keongkido	
Korea	Seo Jeong-nam	531-29, Sinrim-dong, Kwanak-gu, Seoul, Korea	
Korea	Shim Eui-pyo	990-22, Siheung I-dong, Keumcheongu, Jeongdo Twinville 101-801, Seoul. Korea.	
Korea	Shin Dong-myeong	601, Hyundae Apt, 171-61, Bulgwang2-dong, Eunpyong-gu, Soeul, 123-042, Korea	Vice President
Korea	Shin Hyun-sook	309-504, Jugong the 3rd Apt. Myungcheon dong, Boryung City, Chung-Nam, Korea.	
Korea	Shin Soon-ae	695-3, Ahyeon2-dong, Mapo-gu, Seoul city, 121-861, Korea	
Korea	Son Soon-ja	178-2, Sangyeon 1st-dong, 25 Setgolgil, Dongdoocheon, Geongigido, Korea.	Director
Korea	Song Kyung-deok	102-704, Eongbu-Centreville, Wolgyedong, Gwangsangu, Gwangju City.	
Korea	Song Yeon-ju	101-608, Hyundae Apt. Muakdong, Jongnogu, Seoul, Korea.	

Nation	Name	Domicile	Position
Korea	Tae Dong-chul	741-7, Oeri, Youngheungmyeon, Ongjingun, Incheon Metropolitan City, Korea.	
Korea	Won Eung-soon		Director of International Culture & Exchange
Korea	Yang Ah-rim		
Korea	Yang Chi-joong	13 Sudong-gil, Daegu-myun, Kangjin-gun, Jeon-Nam, Korea	
Korea	Yang Hai-wan	508, 101dong, Hangang Apt, Hyoja 3ga-dong, Wansan-gu, Jeonju-city, Jeon-buk, 560-243, Korea	
Korea	Yang Seung-bon	836, Sanghyeon-dong, Suji-gu, Yongin-si, Gyeong-gi-do, 448-130, Korea	
Korea	Yeo Han-kyung	505, wubang town 5dong, 240, hwanggeum 1dong, suseong-gu, Daegu city	
Korea	Yeom Hae-sook	154-1, Rongseong1-dong, Seo-gu, Gwangju-city, 502-810, Korea	
Korea	Yoo Hee-bong	Tel: 02-6412-0702/ 010-6412-0702	
Korea	Yoo Hee-Jeong	104-405, daerim Apartment 57, umyeon-dong, seocho-gu, Seoul, Korea	Director
Korea	Yoon Hyoung-soon	Hyundae Prime Apt. 207-501, Sinjeong-maeul, 2-dong, Pungdeokcheon, Suji-gu, Yongin City, Gyeonggi-do, Korea	
Korea	Yoon Jae-myung		
Korea	Yoon Sang-hyun	713 Sungsa-dong, e-Pyeonhan-Sesang 117-1301, Deokyang-gu, Goyang City, Kyunggi-do	
Korea	Yun Mu-jee	202-705 Yulgok-Ro, Yonkron-dong, Jaeil Office-Tel, Jongno-gu, Seoul	
Korea	Yun Seok-tae	441-1, Seongduri, Gochangeup, Gochanggun, Jeon-Buk, Korea.	
Korea	Yun Sa-weol	Keongsusa, seodangchon, yeonhwari, syimwon-meon, gochanggun, Jeonbuk	
Korea	Yun Su-a	115-902, Hyundae HillState, 155, Onsudong, Gurogu, Seoul, Korea	Director of Public Information

Nation	Name	Domicile	Position
Algerie	El'm Chalbedera	Cité les 160 logements Bât. D3,n 21 2700 Mostaganem Algerie(Africa)	President of Algerie Branch office
Angola	David Mestre	Caixa Postal 10.719 Luanda-Angola(Africa)	President of Angola Branch office
Austaralia	Joy Beadette Cripps	3 Mill St.Aspendale 03 580 415P Australia	President of Australian Branch office
Argentina	Viorginia Rhodas	Rivadavia 2284-1034-Buenos Aires Argentina. Tel.952-2625.(Sud America)	President of Argentina Branch office
Brazil	Olga de Brito	Rua Minas Gerals 65 Jardim Taruma 13200 Jundiai São Paulo, Brazil(Sud America)	President of Brazil Branch office
Brazil	Angela Maria Rocha de Biase	Endereço Av. Silvio Sciumbata, ne 596-Interlagos 04789-010 Såopoulo/Brazil	Vice President of WPRI (charged in South America)
Bulgaria	Dr.Gueni G.Zaimof	(P.E.N)(W.P.S.I) Cokiche 5 Sofia 1421 Bulgaria(East Europe)	President of Bulgaria Branch office
Bosnia and Herzegovina	Ajsa zahirovic.	Str.Kranjcevica 41/3 Sarajevo 71000, Republic Bosnia and Herzegovina(East Europe).	President of Bonia&Herzegovina Branch office
Canada	Stephen Gill	Box 32 932-2135 Cornwall, Ontario K6H 5129 Canada(North America)	President of Canada Branch office
Chille	Desenka Vucasovic de Drasler	Casilla 247. Enap. Cerro Sombrero. Pcia de Tierra del Fuego.X Ⅱ . Region de Magallanes y Antartica Chilena. Chile(Sud America.)	President of Chille Branch office
China P.R	Prof. Lu Jin	Chinese New Poetry Research Insistute South-West-China Normal University Beibei, Chonquing 630715. P.R. China	President of China P.R. Branch office
Colombia	Enrique Osorio Beltran	Calle 131 #45-55 Bogota, D.C., Colombia Tel. (57) (1) 258-01-84	President of Colombia Branch office
Czecho-Slovakia	Vladimir Kostiha	Sekaniny 10805/70800 Ostrava-Poruba Slovakia(Czchoslovakia) (East Europe)	President of Czecho Slovakia Branch office
Denmark	Esther Gress	Ny Strandvej 27 3050 Humlebaek Denmark(Europe)	President of Denmark Branch office
England	Dame Stella Browning	2 Highfield Sussex Road. New Romney, Kent TN 28 8DS England. (Europe) Tel. 0797-363819	President of England Branch office
France	René Streiff	"Close Jean" 1.Rue Marc de Saint-Hilaire/ 83200 Toulong, France. Tel. 94 24 38 94 (Europe)	President of France Branch office
France	Paul Cariage	34. Chemin de Malpeigne 84000 Avignon, France.(Europe)	Vice President of WPRI(charged in Euprope

Nation	Name	Domicile	Position
Germany	Tily Boesche Zachrow	Launinsteig 14 a W-1000 Berlin 28 Germany(west). (Europe)	President of Germany Branch office
Ghana	Larweh Tereson Cofie	C/O The Mirror Graphic Corporation P.O.Box 742. Accra, Ghana, West Africa	President of Ghana Branch office
Grecce	Nickolas Moshovos	Pausania 21, ANO Tumpa GR-54352 The saloniki Greece	President of Greece Branch office
Guatemalak	Cesar Augusto de Leon Morales	Apdo Postal Num 22 13901 Huehretenango Guatemala Central America	President ofGuatemala Branch office
Italy	Giulio Palumbo	M.Cipoia 48 90123 Palermo Italia	President of Italy Branch office
Israel	Dr. Ada Aharoni	57 Horev Haifa Israel 34343 E-MAIL:ADA@ TX.Technion. Ac.IL Israel/Tel-Fax:972-4,824-3230	Vice President of WPRI(charged in Middle East)
Japan	Eiji Kuroha	653-8 Higashigoiso, Oiso-machi Naga-kun kanagawa-Prefequre Japan	President of Japan Branch office
Japan	Uemoto Masao	1-14-34 Kuninobu Umeda-cho Hiroshima-ken Angei-gun 736 Japan	Vice President of WPRI(charged in Asia)
Japan	Yoshifumi Sakura	3-50-8, Koinaka, Nishi-ku, Hiroshima, 733-0813, Japan	
Kwait	Oormila Vijayakrishnan	C/O. K.V. Vijayakrishnan Mechanical Engineer Kwait Fire Service Directorate Serveces Dept. Workshop Complex P.B.No 22228 Safat 13083-Safat, Kwait (Middle East Asia)	President of Kwait Branch office
Latvia	Janis Medenis	Latvian Center P.E.N Box 498 S-10126 Stockholm, Sweden (Europe)	President of Latvin Branch office
Malasia	Chew Khing-Hong	202-A, Jalan Junid, 84000 Muar, Johar, Malaysia. Tel. 06-9511643	President of Malasia Branch office
Malta	Amante Buotempo	J.U.O., Adv. S.R.R. 55st. Paul Street, Valleta VLT 07 Malta. Tel. 22 4082	President of Malta Branch office
Mexico	Elia Domenzain	Prolongacion 5 De Mayo 11 Pueblo San Pedro Martir, Tlalpan 14650, Mexico	President ofMexico Branch office
NewZealand	Anandathana Veronica Haunhey	2B, 'Waikite' Flats,255, the Terace, Wellington, New zealand.	President ofNew Zealand Branch office
Pakistan	Anandaghana Aripirala Viswam	3-6-415/2, 111 Floor, Street-4 Himalyatnagar, Hyderabad-500 029 P	President of Pakistan Branch office
Peru	Mario Rulz De Castilla J.R.	Urbanizacion Magisterial Segunda Etapa-"G" N°.8.Ciudad del Cusco Peru-South America.	President of Peru Branch office
Poland	Bogumil Wtorkievcz	Karczowkowska 12m. 127, 25-019, Kieke, Poland.	President of Poland Branch office

Nation	Name	Domicile	Position
Portugal	Luis Filipe Soares	Apardado 21 208-1131 Lisboa Codex, Portugal.	President of Portugal Branch office
Puerto Rico	José O. Colon Ruiz	P.O.Box 1373 Eaguas Puerto Rico 00626	President of Puerto Rico Branch office
R.O.C	Tin-Wen Chung (R.O.C)	(Continental Regent & Parnasian Jurist respectively) P.O.Box No.58508. Taipei, R.O.C.	President of R.O.C Branch office
Romania	Florentin Smarandache	The Paradoxist Movement P.O.Box 42561 Phoenix, AZ 85080 USA. Tel. (602)436-3862	President of Romania Branch office
Russia	Dr. Adolf P. Shvedchikov	4317 Petit Avenue Encino CA 91436-3516, U.S.A.	Russian Scientist, Poet and translator
Singapore	John L. Chin	# 05-315 Block 978 Jurong West St. 93 Singapore 2264. Tel. 02-7918382	President of Singapore Branch office
Sweden	Martin Allwood	Anglo-American Center S-56532 Mullsjo, Sweden USE.	President of Sweden Branch office
Switzerland	Charles P. Marie	78 Chemin de la Montagne, 1224 Chene-Bougeries, Geneve, Switzerland.	President of Switzerland Branch office
Tunis	Dr. Mohamed Selmi	Villa XYILigue Fu 17 XY, rue Mohamed Beyram 5, 1.004 El-Menzah 5 Tunis	Vice President of WPRI(charged in Africa)
Thailand	Montri Umavijani	14/18 Soi Amporn 6. Gardenhome Village Pabolyothin K,M,26,Bangkok 12130. Thailand	President of Thai Branch office
Uruguay	Alma Vasconcellos	Carlos de la Vega 4383 C.P.11.900 Montevideo Uruguay-Sud America	President of Uruguay Branch office
U.S.A	Park, Meen-Heum	2980 Valentine Ave # 307, Bronx NY 10458, U.S.A	English version Translator
U.S.A	Panos Demetrios	University of Toledo, Toledo, Ohio 43606 U.S.A.	President of U.S.A Branch office
U.S.A.	Teresinka Pereira	P.O.Box 352048 Toledo, OH 43635-2048, U.S.A.	Vice President(char-ged in North America
Venezuela	Max E. Perez	Calle Sucre No. 40 San Fernando-Apture Venezuela (Sud America)	President of Venezula Branch office

Korea / Yeo Ok

(BC~)

Do Not Cross The River

Do not cross the river, I pray.
But should you dare, my dear,
To plunge into water and to death,
What can I do, alas, my dear?

* This song, written in Old Chosun, is known as Konghu-in, a song accompanied by the Konghu, a string instrument. It is said that its author, Yeo-ok, wife of Kwakri-Jago, wrote it from a tale told by her husband.

麗 玉 / 韓國(古朝鮮)

公無渡河歌(箜篌引)

公無渡河
公竟渡河
墮河而死
公將奈何

— 古今注(晋 · 崔豹)所載 —
— 海東繹史記載 —
麗玉 = 津吏 · 霍里子高妻
— 白首老人隨河而死, 麗玉悲感作詩歌 —

공무도하가(공후인)

임은 건너지 말 것이지
임은 물을 건너다가
물에 빠져 죽으시니
임은 마침내 어이하리오

China/Li Bai
(AD. 701-762)

李 白 / 中國(唐)

公無渡河歌

黃河西來決昆侖
咆哮萬里解龍門
波滔天,
堯咨嗟

大禹理百川
兒啼不窺家
殺湍堙洪水
九州始蠶麻
其害乃去 茫然風沙

披髮之搜狂而痴 淸晨徑流欲奚爲
旁人不惜
妻止之老
公無渡河
苦渡之墮

虎可搏
河難恁
公果溺死流海湄邽
有長鯨白齒若雪山
公乎公乎挂罥于其間
箜篌所悲竟不還.

樂府詩 - 公無渡河歌 -

China/Li Bai

(AD. 701-762)

公無渡河(임이여 강을 건너지 마오)

黃河강 西로 흘러 昆崙산을 덮치며
萬里 포효로 龍門에 이른다
파도는 하늘에 닿고
堯임금도 탄식하네

禹왕은 百강을 다스리노라
아이가 태어나도 집을 돌볼 줄 모르네
물살을 잡아 洪水를 멈추니
아홉 州는 누에 치고 麻를 심었네
그 水害는 가고 모래바람 자욱하여라

머리 풀어헤친 미친 老人이
새벽 강물에서 뭘 하는고
주위 사람들은 가만 있으나
妻는 老人을 말리네
임이여 강을 건너지 마오
老人은 건너다 빠졌네

범은 때려서 물리칠 수 있으나
강물은 어찌할 수 없네
임은 드디어 빠져 죽어 바다로 흘러가네
雪山같이 커다란 고래이빨
오오 임은 무서운 이빨에 엮어지고
공후소리만 구슬프구나,
임은 돌아오지 않네

詩人 金 正 雄

Cherishing the Memory of the Late Poet, Kim Joung-woong

* The 2nd President of the World Poetry Institute(1994-2013)
* A Member of the Korean Writers' Association
* A Member of the International Pen Club, Korea Headquarters
* Won the Award of the Gaya Golden Crown of the World Poetry Institute
* Won the Award of the World Poetry Laureates from the International Pen Club
* Published the Poetical Anthologies: Anna's Riverside, etc.

The Poet, Kim Joung-woong has provided a great momentum for exchange of the poetic literature and the cultural promotion of the world poets for the last 20years since 1994.

Suddenly, he passed away on 15th Sept. this year, The news of his death filled all of us with deep sorrow, so we prepared this program of euloging his poetic mind and will.

May his soul rest in peace.

김정웅 시인은 1994년부터 20여 년간 세계시문학회를 이끌어오면서 시문학 교류와 문화 창달에 큰 업적을 남기고 지난 9월 15일 타계했다.

본회는 그 뜻을 기리는 마음으로 본지에 특집을 마련하였다.

고인의 명복을 회원 모두와 함께 빈다.

The Swan Dancing On the Lake

When the morning comes at the food of Noryung mountain,
Seven swans dance in a circle
On Nodong lake, where wild animals have joined together.

Looking at it from Sungwhang temple on Moyang castle,
The lake pushes the darkness beyond the valley
And the lake, shining on the lake
Is veiled in a mist.

The group of the swans,
Dancing freely through the blue water
On the silent and gentle lake!

호수에 춤추는 백조

노령산 기슭에 아침이 열리면
아우르는 노동 저수지에
일곱 마리 백조가 윤무한다

모양성 성황사에서 바라보면
저 건너 계곡의 어둠을 털어내고
호수에 비쳐 오는 햇살에
물안개가 피어 오른다

언제나 고요하고 잔잔한 호수
푸른 물결을 헤치며
자유롭게 춤추는 백조 떼!

The Festival for the Rising Sun

The sun, having run through the past one year,
Having thread the silent heaven and earth,
And now soaring brilliantly from the East Sea,

In the unprecedented deep emotion,
The sun of the new millenium
Meets new morning at the end of heaven.

Burning the last frictions, disgrace, conflicts,
And the dregs of collapse and imprecation,
By the lump of the rising sun,

The sun who is opening the new day of new year,
Comes up in the hot passion,
Cleaving the blue eastern sea.

So
Yesterday, the two thousand years have passed,
Today, the new millenium begins
From the rising sun shining brightly through all the world.

해돋이 축제

즈믄 한 해를 헤치고
고즈넉한 천지를 누비며
동해에서 찬란히 솟는 해님

미증유의 벅찬 감동속에
새 천년의 태양이
하늘 자락에서 새 아침을 맞는다

지난 알력과 오욕과 갈등을
붕괴와 저주의 찌꺼기를
떠오르는 햇덩이로 모두 삭이고

지금 막 새날 새해를 여는 해님이
동쪽 푸른 바다를 가르며
뜨거운 정열로 일어선다

그리하여
어제로 여읜 2천 년
오늘로 시작하는 새 천년은
온 누리에 밝게 비치는 해돋이

Anna's Riverside 1

Anna!
She is spinning around the riverside
Like a whirlwind.

She looks as if getting caught,
But not seized by hands.

Now at the hill over the riverside
Picking up a handful of peach blossoms
She floats one petal or two
On the bluer river.

The more I alienate Anna far away from me,
The more she drags over my heart,

The more I approach nearer to her,
The more she gets rid of me from my bosom.

안나의 강변 1

안나!
안나는 돌개바람같이
강변을 빙빙 돌고 있다.

잡힐 듯 잡힐 듯하면서도
손아귀에 꼭 지어지지 않는다.

지금도 강변 저 언덕에선
도화꽃을 한 움큼 따 들고
푸르디푸른 강물에
한 잎 두 잎 띄우고 있다.

멀리 안나를 잃어버리려고 하면
내 마음에 와 꽉 닿고

안나와 가까이 하려고 하면
내 품에서 헤어나 통그라지는 것 같다.

Anna's Riverside 6
- Love Song of Kyungpodae 2

At the foggy Kyungpodae
When the water-fowls cry,
The love by its riverside rolls about.

When they blow on the wing,
The boats that are crossing the sea
Make white bubbles.

When the bell-sound of Han Maek rings at noon,
Walking along the riverside,
We whisper a legend like flowery cloud to each other.

A white sailing vessel
Appears from the far horizon
Merging into the blue sky,

In our heart
That we are looking at
The love is curdled.

안나의 강변 6

-경포대 연가 2

안개어린 경포대에
물새가 지저귀면
그 바닷가 사랑이 출렁인다

그 물새 날으면
바다를 가로지르는 보트는
하얀 포말을 이룬다

한 맥(脈)의 종소리 정오를 울릴 때
해변을 거닐며
꽃구름 전설을 속삭인다

푸른 하늘과 맞닿는
저 멀리 수평선에서
흰 돛단배가 보이고

그 배를 바라보는
우리들의 가슴에는
사랑이 어리고 있다.

An Ideal Woman 1
- The Woman like Yellow Soil

The woman like yellow soil, so abundant, richly tasteful
As to be mixed in red and yellow soil,
Who has been symbolized as our natural dyes,

She is one who dyes Korean costumes, Korean paper, soaps,
And ceramic wares in yellow soiled color of natural dyes,
Drawing out fragrance and beauty.

The old-fashioned, elegant woman,
Wearing deep yellow soiled scarf,
Tying a coat string with her head down modestly,

Will she be a Koryo woman
Or will she be a Chosun woman?
She is a beautiful woman smiling with yellow soiled color
And with a figure as elegant as a fairy.

이상형(理想鄕)의 여인 1
- 황토의 여인

풍요롭고 덕성스런 감칠맛 나는 황토
빨강, 노랑 흙을 혼합한 것처럼
천연물감으로 나타나는 황통의 여인

생활한복 한지 비누 도자기에
황토색깔로 천연염색을 하여
향기와 아름다움을 어울려 내는 여인

황토의 짙은 스카프를 쓰고
옷고름 여미며 다소곳이 고개 숙인
고풍이 흐르는 정숙한 여인

고려의 여인일까?
조선의 여인일까?
선녀처럼 우아한 자태에
황토빛 미소짓는 아름다운 여인.

An Ideal Woman 3

- A Balmy Breeze Melting the Lingering Snow

On a gentle breeze of the winter season
Her voice longing to hear
Is heard beyond Byunsan sea as the wind voice

Hearing about Soyo monk' mythology very interesting,
Between every auspicious valley and hill of Soyo
Under the clear and blue sky without a cloud,
With what sort of flower is my heart touched?

You take a red glass,
And I have a delicious looking glass of fruit wine,
Together we toast our eternity.

Our love, first beginning from Agape,
That has never repentance,
At last carries us to Eros with Psyche
The legend, involved in every mossy stone
With the electric lights of Moyang castle to shine,
Touches my heartstrings more in a half moon's emotion.

이상향의 여인 3
- 잔설을 녹이는 훈풍

겨울철 모처럼의 훈풍에
그립고 아쉬움의 목소리
저 건너 변산바다 바람으로 들려온다

잔설을 녹이는 소요 대사의 신화를 들으며
소요산 계곡과 기슭 기슭마다 서기 어리는
티 한 점 없는 맑고 푸르른 하늘 아래
무슨 꽃으로 문지르는 가슴인가?

그대는 붉으레한 글라스를 들고
나는 자양분 넘치는 복분자 잔을 들고
사랑의 영원을 건배 한다

애초에 플라토닉한 아가페에서
사랑은 결코 후회하지 않는
프쉬케와 더불어 에로스에 이른다

어둠을 밝히는 모양성의 전광은
이끼 낀 돌 하나하나에 얽힌 전설이
반월의 정념에 더욱 심금을 울린다.

The Flower of Reciprocal Love 2
- An Echo Sinking into the Heart

The petal burning redly
Means an unrequited love, yearning each other
Revealed by Dosol.

It's an echo sinking into the heart
To the lover, burning its passion
In the splendidly flowered temple on the mountain.

Ah.....the flower of mutual love, that is blooming brilliantly!
With their sad stories carved on every petals,
Shall it sing the lover's song today?

상사화 2

-사무치는 메아리

붉게 타오르는 꽃잎
도솔의 계시는 받아
서로 그리다 등진 짝사랑

흐드러지게 핀 산사에
정열을 태우면서
님을 향해 사무치는 메아리

아…… 현란히 피는 상사화여!
꽃잎 잎마다 슬픈 사연을 새기어
오늘도 구원의 노래를 부르려나.

The World Poet's Meeting
- Istanbul of Turkey

When the flower of a marronnier blooms in the old castle,
Its young buds under the sunshine
Are wet with bright dews.

From the third palace of the Osman Age
With the waves billowing near its Golden Hall,
The Bosporus bridge stands far away.

The Palace of Dolmabahce in middle of 1800 years
Is a elegant and majestic architecture in Honper style
With a crystal chanjeria.

Along the small road between the stone walls
There stand 'Pierotte Cafes' of the nameless military officer.

* Pierrotte Cafe: When an French military officer stayed in Istanbul, Turkey, he fell in love with a charming woman, with aa big dream of future, returned his home country, and again came back to Istanbul to meet her, but he found she died to bury into the grave, so in crying for her and calling her name, he also died of lovesickness. In memory of his love, the Pierrotte Cafe called his name in this place.

세계 시인대회
-터키의 이스탄불

고성에 마로니에 꽃이 필 때
햇볕에 튕기는 꽃망울
영롱한 이슬을 머금고 있다

오스만 시대의 세 번째 궁전
골든 홀에 드리우는 물결
저 멀리 보스포러스 다리가 있다

천팔백 년 중엽 돌마바흐체 궁전은
장엄하고 우아한 흔퍼식 건물
수십 톤의 금은과 상제리아와 크리스탈

성벽 돌담길 사이사이
가신님의 무덤 앞에 슬피 울다 쓰러진
이름 없는 무관의 *"피에롯트" 카페, 카페

*피에롯트 카페: 한 프랑스 무관이 터키 이스탄불을 집정할 때 어느 여인과 눈이 맞아 황홀한 꿈을 갖고 퇴직 후 잠시 귀국했다 돌아와 보니 이미 그 여인은 죽어 무덤에 묻히게 되어 그녀를 울부짖으며 너무나 그리워 하다가 상사병으로 죽은 그 자리에 그의 이름의 카페가 들어서게 되었다.

Mongol

- In the Literary Exchange Between Korea and Mongol

If we move up to the east of Asia
Snooping around,
A small fine Country in the upper part of the Korean Peninsula
Is seen in the dazzling sun.

Genghis Khan of Mongol
Howls at this world,
Galloping a horse all over the world
In the sands and wide fields of the continent.

Through the Mongol's spot
His spirit is inherited down
To this beautiful Korea
Along the coast of the West sea.

Ah! over the friendly bridging between Korea and Mongol
The sound of the culture, language, and peace
Is heard so sonorously, that it is sowed as the seed of literature,
Flapping the flag of the lyric poetry.

한-몽 문학교류
- 세계시문학회

아세아의 동쪽으로
기웃기웃 올라가면
아담한 한반도의 끝
태양빛에 눈이 부시다

사막과 허허벌판 대륙에서
온 누리에 말을 달리며
세계를 포효하는
몽골의 징기스칸

서해의 연안을 타고
금수강산 화려한 나라에
몽골반점의 증표로
이어주고 있다

아! 서정시의 깃발을 날리며
세계의 문화 언어 평화
한-몽 문학의 씨를 뿌려
친선의 가교가 낭랑히 들려온다.

The Southern Island of New Zealand

- The National Park, Piordland

Every place the mountainside touches each other,
Lots of lakes flow down
And at the end of lakes extending down,
12 bays of the sea lean on them.

The countless mountain peaks,
The water course pouring down the rockwalls,
And about hundred meters of silk streams of waterfall
Dance in a circle like a nymph's skirt.

At every foot of a rock mountain,
Tens of the thread of the waterfalls
Form a great one
And fall down to the lake and the sea in a grand sound.

뉴질랜드 남섬
- 피오르드랜드 국립공원

산자락이 닿는 곳마다
수많은 호수가 흐르고
길게 뻗어 내리는 호수 끝에
열두 개의 바다 만(灣)이 깃대어 있다

헤일 수 없는 산봉우리
암벽을 타고 내리는 물줄기
백여 미터의 명주비단이
요정의 옷자락처럼 윤무한다

바위 산 기슭마다
수십의 실줄기 폭포는
대폭포가 되어 웅장한 소리로
호수와 바다에 떨어진다.

Australia
- The Blue Mountain

All mountains are formed in climbing them,
But the Blue Mountain is formed as only one property in the world
That upper part forms ground, lower part mountain,
Because its base is very weak in going down.

The red mountain is rich in iron and gold,
And the black one is deposited plentifully underground,
Where the forest fire has broken out
By the evening dew in ultraviolet rays.

The blue colored haze
Is a phenomenon presented in refracting
The oil-stained grain by the sunlight,
Emanating from the rubber tree.

호주

- 블루마운틴

모든 산은 오르면서 산이 형성된다
그러나 지반이 약하므로
내려가면서 상지하산(上地下山)이 발생하는
블루마운틴이라는 세계유산의 호주

철과 금이 풍부한 붉은 산과
석탄이 매장돼 있는 검정 산
이 곳은 자외선 기운으로
저녁이슬이 산불을 자주 내기도 한다

푸른 빛 아지랑이는
고무나무에서 발산하는
기름성분의 알갱이에
햇빛이 굴절되어 나타나는 현상.

Cambodia

- Angkorwatt

The antique-looking Hindoo's Top as an ancient castle,
Is one of the 7 mysteries in the world,
Is built up for 200 years, one thousand years ago.

The main palace built up at the sun-rising East
And made the front gate at the sunset.

The 1st floor of lower classes is the common people,
The 2nd floor of present state is equivalent to middle classes,
And the 3rd floor of heavenly state is the royal family and monks as special class.

Ascending its stairs toward the clockwise
With an incline of 45 degrees,
The cardinal points stretches crossroads.

Their skill for masonry with the artistic soul
Is mysterious beyond our imagination,
Showing it at the Ancor Angkorwatt in this century.

캄보디아
- 앙코르와트

고색이 창연한 힌두교의 탑
세계 7대 불가사이로
천 여 년 전 200년간 쌓은 옛 성

태양이 솟는 동쪽에 본궁을 쌓고
해가 지는 서쪽에 돌탑 정문을 냈다

미물계의 1층은 평온한 서민층
현상계의 2층은 중간 계급층
천상계의 3층은 왕족과 승려의 특별 계급층

45도 가파른 경사 층층에
시계 방향으로 거슬러 올라가면
동서남북이 십자가로 뻗어 있다

예술 혼을 담은 석공 기법은
인간으로 도저히 상상할 수 없는
금세기의 신비로운 앙콜 앙코르와트.

Egypt of the Ancient Civilization
- The Capital City of Cairo

Cairo, meaning victory in Arabian language
Is the biggest city in Africa as a capital city.
Through which the Nile was passing,
The newborn Mosses drifting down in an ark of bulrushes
To escape Pharaoh's persecution was saved by Pharaoh's daughter.

Cairo, the capital city, from the nations of Egyptian civilization
Was called 'Misrue in Arabian name,
And its eastern hill was named 'Alcaliobia',
The western coast 'Alija Alcaliobia',
So it is well harmonious in the Ancient and Modern,
In the tradition, the Orient and the West.

The capital city of its civilization with more 6 thousand years of history,
Stretched widely to the left side of Nile River from Gejira Island,
But the city showed us the declining social institutions
Due to the increasing overpopulation and poverty.

The Nile River passing through the central city
Is the original source to bloom an Egyptian civilization,
And also the mother's breast of the Egyptian civilization ever.

고대 문명의 이집트
-이집트 수도 카이로

아랍어로 승리를 뜻하는 카이로는 이집트 수도
아프리카에서 손꼽히는 가장 큰 도시
헤롯왕의 재난을 피하기 위해
바구니에 실려 나일 강을 떠내려 오는 모세는
빨래하는 여인에 의해 건져 진다

이집트 문명의 중심권에서
카이로는 '미스르' 라는 아랍 이름으로 불리우며
동쪽 언덕은 알칼리오비야
서안은 알지자 알칼리오비야에 걸쳐있고
전통과 동서의 영향, 고대와 현대가 잘 조화된 도시

이집트 게지라 섬에서 나일 강 왼쪽 언덕에 뻗쳐있어
6천 년 이상의 역사를 가진 문명의 수도
그러나 늘어만 가는 인구 팽창과 가난으로
쇠락해 가는 사회기관 시설을 동시에 보여 준다

시가(市街) 중앙을 뚫고 흐르는 나일 강은
이집트 문명을 꽃피운 원천이며
지금도 변함없이 이집트의 젖줄이기도 하다.

A Pussy Willow

The pussy willow,
Opening up the frozen brook
Wiggling for the first time, breaking the Spring News,

The little hairy pepper,
Forming whitely on the every end of twigs
With the Spring Message,

The pussy willow along the brook
Spreading the spring fragrance
More than that of the golden bells and azaleas,

If it's not the pussy willow,
Who will break the Spring Fragrance
So early to us?

버들강아지

개울 얼음을 털고
최초로 바들거리며
봄소식을 알리는 버들강아지

봄의 전령을 싣고
버들가지 가지 끝마다
하얗게 맺히는 작은 털 고추

개나리, 진달래보다
봄의 향기를 먼저 풍기는
개울가 버들개지

유서(柳絮) 아니라면
뉘라서 봄의 훈향을
그렇게 빨리 알릴 것인가?

* 유서: 버들개지를 말함.

ODE TO THE LIVING

- To the Memory of Indira Gandhi

We are all puppets
Of her - Time,
Our hands and feet

Tied to her apron-strings of Fate.

We are all babes
Of her - Dame Reality
Our lips and tongues
Glued to her iron nipples.

We are all slaves
Of him Emperor Karmah
You, me and they
We all serve him night and day.

And we are all prisoners
Of her - Mother Earth
For our sins and vices
We come and go serving Time.

Larweh Therson Cofie / Africa

The MIRROR
P.O.BOX 742, ACCRA, GHANA Africa

삶에 부치는 송가
- 안디라 간디의 추모에 부침

우리는 모두 꼭두각시다,
그녀 시대의
우리 손과 발은

그녀의 손수건에 묶인 채 - 운명의 실이리라

우리는 모두
그녀의 애기이다 - 진실의 귀부인
우리 입술과 혀는
그녀의 쇠 젖꼭지에 붙어 있다.

우리는 모두
그의 노예다 - 운명의 황제
너, 나 그리고 그들과
우리 모두는 밤, 낮으로 그를 받든다.

그리고 우리 모두는
그녀의 죄수이다 - 어머니 땅
우리 모두의 죄와 악을 위해
우리는 와서 시간을 모시러 간다.

Embroider my hair with Seashells

Embroider my hair with seashells,
with pale sand my shoulders, yes.
I don't ask for kisses, don't you think of cares:
only nature in your gesture and eyes.
The open fields I never abide
but white sea caves -
stalactitcs and salt.
The ground sand aches for cold and lonely,
rosy opals surround and preserve me.
Provide my feet, if you want,
with reed sandals,
but in the routes of the world
I won't impress my footsteps;
although in all places I have my thinking,
my senses in whatever harbor or home.
Only, to conquests I don't surrender,
from the pure water strands I don't stray,
clean from love and evil.
Come from a ship, no matter who you are
and, beside me, sit, if you wish;
but, for me, don't dream of dawns,
only pour on me flowers
of seashells and sand.

Irene De Melloneves/Brazil

Caixa postal 2016
30.000-Belo Horizonte Minas Gerais Brazil

나의 머리를 조가비로 수놓아라

나의 머리를 조가비로 수놓아라.
나의 어깨는 창백한 모래로 수놓아라.
나의 키스를 요구하지 않겠다. 걱정말고
너의 태도와 눈속에 본성만을 생각해라.
나는 결코 열려 있는 들판에 머물 수 없지만
종유석과 소금으로 된 흰 바다의 동굴에 머물 수 있으리.
모래사장은 차갑고 쓸쓸히 아치를 이루고
장미빛 오팔은 나를 둘러싸고 보호하고 있으니.
네가 원한다면 나의 발에 갈대신발을 신겨주라.
그러나 세상의 행로마다
나는 발자국을 남기지 않으리;
비록 모든 곳에서 내가 생각하고
어떤 항구나 집에서 감각을 지닌다 할지라도
단지 정복하기 위해서 나는 굴복하지는 않으리.
깨끗한 바닷가도 배회하지 않으리.
사랑과 악으로부터 청소되어,
네가 누구든지간에 배로부터 나와라.
그리고 내옆에 앉아라. 네가 바란다면.
하지만 나를 위해 새벽녘의 꿈은 꾸지마라.
오로지 나에게 조가비와 모래의 꽃을 쏟아부어라.

The Citadel of our Dreams

The citadel of our dreams
Looms behind
A Rose intertwined
With another Rose

A loving couple
In the foreground
Of our blank page

Exit from the shadows
The sculpture
Maps our future.

Hédi Bouraoui/Canada

4700 Keele Street
North York
Ontario, Canada M3J 1P3

우리 꿈의 성(城)

우리 꿈의 성채는
다른 장미와 뒤엉킨
한 송이 장미 뒤에
희미하게 보인다.

우리의 비어 있는 책장 속의
정원 속에 있는
사랑의 연인들은

그림자로부터 퇴장한다.
그 조각품이
우리의 미래를 그려놓는다.

MIS FUNDAMENTOS

Ninguna otra miel,
solamente la del conocimiento.
Ninguna otra luz,
únicamente la de la sabiduria.
Ningún otro propósito,
sino el de la curiosidad.
Ninguna otra búsqueda,
sino la del pensamiento riguroso.
Ningún otro viaje,
sino el de los libros,
a través de cuyas páginas
todo es iluminado
y adquiere el sabor
del más dilecto manjar dionisiaco.

ENRIQUE OSORIO BELTRAN / Colombia

*Born in Bogota, Colombia, in 1958.
*Writer, Poet, Philosopher and Astronomer.
*Member of several international associations.
*His poems are in several anthologies of many countries.
*Received 3 st. Prize, XII Concurso de Poesia "El paisaje", Aranguren, Vizcaya, Spain, 1983; 1 st.Prize, Concurso Poetico "Nirvana Populi", Segovia, Spain, 1983. Titles: Titular Academico, Vizcaya, Sapin, 1978; Academico Benemerito ad Honorem, Felgueiras, Portugal, 1981; Honorary Appointment to "The research Board of advisors, 1999, American Biographical Institute, USA. President for Colombia of World Poetry Research Institute of Korea.
*Address: Calle 131 #45-55 BOGOTA, D.C., COLOMBIA
* Tel: (57) (1) 258 01 84 / H.P.(Celular): 3204764752
*E-mail: enosbe@hotmail.com

SUTILEZA Y ENCANTO

Sutileza y encanto,
vida que hallas en la lluvia,
manantial de frescura,
ojos abiertos a los suenos
y cordilleras plenas de verano;
atardecer que de sombras mágicas
va trajeando el día,
va enalteciendo el alma
con sus arpegios líricos,
en sus instantes de oro,
acordes de violín,
Paganini eterno
en la viajera nube blanca
de los más tempranos sueños.
Sutileza y encanto,
¡ oh acústica miel de la poesia
y del más profundo conocimiento!

Give what you like

Since I have saved your life
in the maze of the Seven Wells
you can give what you like:
a rose from the sands
a jasmine flower
the sweetness from palms
of from the leaves of mint,
the flesh of the coconut tree
or camel's milk,
or simply your smile
as bright as the sun that shines
on the cool oasis.
But,
if you have nothing to give
no flower, no fruit, no joy,
nothing at all,
I understand

Jacqueline Thévoz / England

네가 좋아하는 것을 주어라

내가 너의 生命을 구한 이래
일곱 개의 벽으로 된 미궁속에서
너는 네가 좋아하는 것을 줄 수 있다.
모래밭으로부터 한 떨기 장미를
한 송이 재스민 꽃을
종려나무나 박하잎으로부터 달콤함을
코코아나무의 신선함을
낙타의 우유를
혹은 시원한 오아시스에 비치는 태양처럼
밝고 순박한 너의 미소를
하지만,
네가 만일 아무것도 줄 것이 없다면
꽃도, 과일도, 기쁨도
전혀 아무것도 없더라도
나는 이해한다.
그리고 부탁한다. 네가 타오르는 나의 손에
한 방울의 눈물이나마 떨어뜨리길.

Old Acquaintance

I met my teenage self the other day;
She stepped out the note-books that I'd kept
And looked at me accusingly. Except
In trivialities, there was no way
I'd played the part that she had meant to play.
Hers was a mind unwilling to accept
That dreams could fail, or people prove inept,
Or good intentions suffer feet of clay.
My struggling protestations seemed uncouth.
Contrasted with the simple clarity
With whch her innocence expressed the truth.
The only sign of progress seems to be
That, whereas I admire my clear-eyed youth,
Her understanding couldn't stretch to me.

M.E.Spain/England

Flat 34 Airile House
17 Airlie Gardens LONDON
W8 7AN

오랜 사귐

나는 언젠가 나 자신의 십대(拾代) 시절을 만났다.
그녀는 내가 보관했던 공책을 들고 걷고 있었고
나를 나무라듯 보고 있었다.
사소한 것을 제외하고는
그녀가 연기하고자 했던 부분들을
내가 연기할 수 있는 방법은 없었다.
실패했던 꿈들, 또는 인간이 바보라는 것,
좋은 의도가 점토 속에 빠져 고통받는다는 사실을
받아들이고 싶지 않은 마음이었다.
나의 도전적인 항의는
진실을 표현하는 그녀의 순수하고 단순한 명백함과
비교하여 볼 때 투박한 것으로 보였다.
발전과 진보의 단 하나의 표시는
내가 맑은 눈의 젊음을 찬미하는데 비해
그녀의 이해가 나에 미칠 수 없음에 있는 듯 했다.

A Tattoo

I get up at dawn
And open a day freshly.

Though the coldness
Coming with original sin is fearful,

Making my heart warm up in a cup of tea
And patch the broken minds on,

The scars, stitched more than hours left alone
Rather has a pain to me.

They are not mine,
And not yours,

So this morning,
In your name

Bae Young-suk/Korea

* Born in Suncheon, Jeonnam.
* The Manager of Soonchеon branch office, A teacher at Kwangyang middle school.
* Published two Poetical Anthologies: 'The Poor Seoul', 'Yearning is Hanging down from White Cotton Curtain'
* baenara@hanmail.net
* http://blog. daum.net/ baenara

I tattoo our hearts
A stitch by stitch

By an arrowhead
Exchanged many times with each other.

- Tr. by Won Eung-soon

문신

새벽에 일어나
정갈하게 하루를 연다

원죄를 따라오는
냉기가 무섭지만

차 한 잔에 가슴 데워
조각난 마음을 덧대고 나니

방치한 시간보다
꿰맨 자국이 오히려 아파온다

내 것이 아니고
네 것이 아닐 바엔

서로의 심장을
수없이 오가는 화살촉으로

너의 이름으로
이 아침

한 땀 한 땀
문신을 새긴다.

A Picture, Painted in Soil

The dewy strawberries mellowed
And the earth-born wild flowers
Vomit the yellow soil,
And the green color of bamboo is brightly green.

He threw away an oil painting,
The colors, found out through soil,
And softness, held the sun and moon in its bosom,
Flow dimly in the picture.

Over the house wall with the splendid trumpet flowers,
The girl, sending shameful smile
The morning scenery at the bright vineyard
With farmer's sweat is a festival yard.

The hours, sent eyeing the sun and the moon,
And the dewy life are gone with morning sunshine,
The time, peeling off the color in the soil one by one fold,
Was the friend of trees.

Baek Bong-ki/Korea

* Manager of the Central council of Agricultural Cooperated Association in Gochang District.
* Address : 103, 116dong, Hyundae apt, ajung-ri, Inhu1-dong, Deokjin-gu, Jeonju-si, Jeon-buk, 561-781, Korea.

The wild landscapes, completed in colors of its own soil,
And his life, sought after the Pharaoh's golden mask is bright.

*At an exhibition of artist, Cho Do-joong

- Tr. by Won Eung-soon

흙으로 그린 그림

이슬 먹은 산딸기가 무르익고
흙을 먹고 자란 야생화는
황토를 토해 내는데
산죽의 초록빛은 청초하다

유화를 던지고 흙을 붙들어
찾아낸 색체들
해와 달을 품었던 포근함이
화폭에서 은은하게 흐르네

능소화 흐드러진 담 너머
수줍은 미소를 던지고 있는 소녀,
농부의 땀방울이 빛나는 포도원
아침 풍경이 축제 마당이다

해와 달과 눈짓하며 흐른 시간들
이슬의 생은 아침햇살에 사라지고
흙속의 색깔 한 겹씩 벗겨내는 시간은
나무들이 벗이었다

흙이 품은 색으로 완성한 야생의 풍경들
파라오의 황금가면을 찾아간 생이 빛난다.

* 조도중 화백의 전시회를 보고

The Field-lane at Early Autumn

Our field, connected for the steep hill-path
To a learning house of the village,
Is the place
Where the mountain's energy is flowing down from every curve,
And the lane is where I had picked up green perilla in former days,
Coming down getting unripe peppers in hands,
Casually, over the far horizontal
From an isle of 'Murg' coming in sight
A fireball glows with twilight in flame.
After the setting sun dyed the west sky and sea with a rosy flush,
Disappeared from the far sea without our knowledge,
Only the waves are rising silently.

- Tr. by Won Eung-soon

Bang Jung-sun/Korea

* Awarded new-poet prize from monthly "Literature and Arts" in 2001.
* Member of the World Poetry Research Institute.
* Address: 360, Jaryong-ri, Sangha-myeon, Gochang-gun, Jeonbuk, 585-910, Korea
Tel: 010-6770-0481

초가을 들길

굽이굽이 산정기 내리는 곳
우리 밭 서당발
가파른 언덕길
그 전날에도 들깻잎 따오던 그 길
풋고추 손에 들고 내려오는 길
무심코 바라보는 머그섬 저 쪽
빨강 불덩이 하나 훨훨 타고 있다
불에 휩싸인 노을까지도
해님은 그렇게 바다와 서쪽 하늘에
곱게 물들여 놓으시고
바다 저 멀리
아무도 모르게 사라진 뒤에
물결만 말없이 일렁입니다.

Petals Fade In the Night Rain

Did my love come and go quietly
leaving his words on every petal?

Did sad love fall down?
Each petal has tears

Blooming flowers at every course of Seomjin River
Wither in the night rain and fall

In the night of falling petals
In the night of falling petals
I went up to the stormy hill

Did love come and go
In a moment like that?

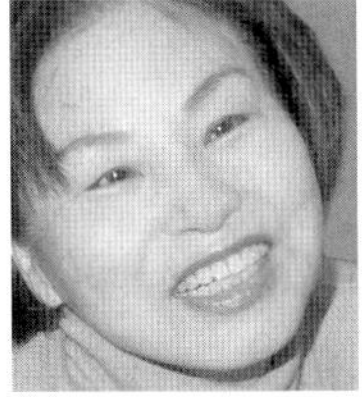

Bark Il-so / Korea

* Awarded a prize for a budding writer from the recommended writer's association
* A member of Korean Writers' Association
* Published joint literary work entitled 'In Autumn, I Want to like the tree'
* Poetic Anthology: The Mind's Mirror under the Flowers; A Letter Sending to Heaven; The Love of Young Years Blooming as An Aquarelle

* Address: 603, 101 dong, Jugong Apt, wolgye 2-dong, nowon-gu, Seoul, Korea
* Tel : H.P 011-9833-3154 * E-mail: barkiso@hanmail.net

Petals wither in the rain and wind
The love in your eyes has gone in the wind and rain
Apple blossoms' smell has gone from your lips

The love turns petals' tears
In the falling rain at night
Its brightness makes me sadder

- Translated by Hongkyu Choe

밤비에 꽃잎 지고

님이 왔다가
소리없이 떠났는가
꽃잎마다
진주로 사연 남겨 놓고

슬픈 사랑이 내렸는가
꽃잎마다
눈물이 맺혀 있다

섬진강 줄기마다
피어나던 꽃잎도
밤비에 져버렸네
떨어져 가네

꽃잎 지던 밤에
꽃잎 지던 밤에
비바람 몰아치던 언덕엘
찾아 갔었네

사랑은 그렇게
한순간 왔다 가는가

비바람에 꽃잎은 지고
그대 눈속에 가득찬 사랑도
비바람에 비어가고
사과꽃 향기 나던 입술에서
향기도 사라지네

Korea/박일소

내리는 밤비에
꽃잎마다 맺힌 눈물로
사라진 사랑
영롱함이 더욱 슬프다

A Picture of Still Life

A picture of still life
As brilliant as the wedding,
That is ripen delicious, day and night.

The noted apples and pears of the East Sea,
With the doll's faces
Adhere to canvas.

At the morning of creation,
The sound of the cock
Surging along the tide,
Is on the wing, sowing a legend.

- Tr. by Won Eung-soon

Cho Ki-hyun/Korea

* Majored in Painting, at College of Fine Arts, Seoul National University.
* Retired from Middle & High School as a Principal.
* Prizes of Han Mak Literature, The Literary Trend, The Space of Literature, and The World Poetry Research Institute.
* Now A Critic, Poet, Essayist, Painter, and A Dancer.
* Address: 102, 5-dong, Hanjung villa, Chunchun-ri, Maesong-myeon, Whasong-si, Gyeonggi-do, Korea.

정물화(靜物畵)

낮과 밤
맛있게 영그는
화혼(華婚)의 정물화

사과, 배 동해의 명작
인형들의 얼굴이
캔버스(canvas)에 밀착된다

창조의 아침
조류(潮流) 따라 밀려오는
계성(鷄聲)의 소리가
전설을 뿌리며 날아간다.

The Day Flying Like a Crane

My soul,
Due to you
Takes after free clouds,

The dreamlike happiness,
Allowed by a karma(destiny)
Without taking pains to get it.

Deliberately
With nothing to be bound,
My soul is free like a wind.

If you
Have the day flying like a crane,
I would become your blue heaven.

- Tr. by Won Eung-soon

Choi Byeong-ryun / Korea

* A member of Jeongeup literary club
* A member of Jeonbuk writer's club
* A director of Baikya Literary men club
* A member of the World Poetry Research Institute
* Started literary carrier (poet) through "Literary Movement & Trend" in 2009
* President of jeongeup branch of Lions Club
* President of jeoneup agent of Hyundai marine insurance
* An adviser of the jeong-eup City Federation for Environmental Movement

그런 날을

당신이 있어
내 영혼은
한가한 구름 닮고

애써 구하지 않았어도
인연 닿아 허락된
꿈 같은 행복

구태여
매일 일 없으니
바람처럼 자유로워

내가 창공이 되고
당신은
학처럼 나는 날을……

A Prosperous Shop

At a corner's shop in a town
Some articles
Are covered with dust,
As much as their thickness, only gaping.

The spectacles for aged and the abacus's bead
Are joined on good terms
With an elderly master
Like old couples.

Two drunken men even in the daytime
At the floor in front of the shop,

Are grasping each other by throat,
Throwing appetizers and the 'Makoly' bottles, as if they vent spites over a person,
Taken a mortgaging on the bowstring of winds.

It sleets heavily
And the dubious eyes of passers-by
Are waving on the signboard.

- Tr. by Won Eung-soon

Choi Hyun-sun / Korea

* Member of the Korean Writers' Association
* Member of Editorial Staff at "The Plus Poems"
* Vice Chairman of "the Literary Club of Nature"
* Director of the Literary Association of the Korea Creative Literature for Reciting Poems
* Member of the Soon-Su Literature, & of the World Poetry Institute
* Address: 541-20 Daeyadong, Siheung City, Kyeonggi Province, Korea
* Mobile-Phone: o10-5689-2155 *E-mail: gustjs2155@daum.net

번창상회

동네 한 구석
몇 안 되는 물건들이
제 두께 만큼의 먼지에 쌓여
하품 한창이다

뿌연 돋보기와 주판알
초로의 주인과 어우러져
의좋게 살아가는
노부부 모습 같다

가게 앞 평상에선
대낮부터 술에 취한 두 남자

새우깡과 막걸리병 집어 던지며
바람의 활시위에 저당 잡힌 한 풀려는 듯
서로 멱살잡이 하고 있다

추적추적 진눈깨비 내리고
지나는 사람들 의아한 눈빛
간판 위에서 출렁댄다

To the Bamboo

I look at you,
The brilliant morning of the snowed bamboo,
And I look at you again.
Even though looking at you
Through all four seasons,
Because I couldn't stand
Instead of you,
How could I fix the day separately.

At this morning of the snowed bamboo,
I look at you again.
O, the Light! soaking into my mind,
O, the clear Sound! being mild,
O, the slender Knuckles! being outstanding,
Raise me up,
Me, me.

- Tr. by Won Eung-soon

Choi Seung-beom/Korea

* Born in Namwon. A poet. A doctor of literature
* A professor emeritus of Cheonbuk Univ.
* A superintendent at Goha Literature attached to Cheonju star bank
* Started a literary career(Korean poem) through Heondai(modern) literature in 1958
* A manager of Cheonju branch office of Korea Writer Association
* Awarded Jeongwun Sijo(Korean poem) literary, Korea Modern poem literary, Garam sijo literary, Korea Literary, Mokjeong Literary, Nation Literary, Korean Poem Literary(in the first bout of its ceremony)
* A literary work : Study on Korean Essay, The Fragrance of Namwon, Virtue and Vice are All My Teacher, Essay about Korean Poem, Flower-A Woman-Times, A Sound etc.
* Poetical works : In front of an Orchid, Nature's Monologue, A Journey to Mongolia, At the Crater Lake on Mt. Paekt, Hiding Myself with a Withered Leaf etc.

대나무에게

설청의 눈부신 아침
너를 바라본다
너를 바라본다
따로 날이 있으랴
사철을
바라보아도
너로 설 수
없는 것을

설청의 이 아침에
너를 다시 바라본다
개운히 스미는 빛이여
성글어 맑은 소리여
빼어난
밋밋한 마디여
부추겨다오
나를 나를

A Citron

When I stand beside the green citron,
It attracts freshly young eyes of mine.
There's no as beautiful as youth in the world.

They say
The rough skin is the same as the citron's,
But only if can take after its fragrance,
Its elastic vitality, and be as young as the citron
Though it looks ugly,
The setting sun hangs in the west as old as my age.

It's a busy wayfarer.

- Tr. by Won Eung-soon

Choi Sun-ae/Korea

- Debuted as poet by Han maek Literature
- Pubisher. Member of Korea Literature Association, The World Poetry Research, Suncheon Literature club, leader of Pilmar Literaler club.
- Address : 489-1 Jekok-dong Suncheon-City Jeonnam 540-110 Korea

유자

청푸른 유자 그 곁에 서면
싱싱한 젊음 눈길 잡아맨다
젊은 만큼 예쁜 것 어디 또 있으랴

못 생긴 사람 피부를 가리켜서
유자껍질 같다지만
풋풋한 향기와 파란 빛의
톡 터질 듯한 생동감
못 생겨도 유자처럼 젊을 수 있다면
그 향기 닮을 수 있다면
서산 해 내 나이 또래쯤 걸려 있다

갈 길 바쁜 나그네

Today and Tomorrow

However hard we may live, we cannot know it,
That to live roaming near death,
Is not easy thing for us.

All through summer in fickle wind,
We stir up the death suspended from plate-scraps.
In the trap full of hubbub
Even though we have led our life until today without future,
I want to confine me opening the door.

Choung Song-jun / Korea

*Born at Uijeongboo, Geonggido, Korea.
*Graduated from Dept. of Jungang Univ. & the Graduate School of Jungang Univ..
*Retired as a Principal of Jukjeon Middle School, Yongin, Geonggido.
*Recommended as a poet from the magazine, "Poetry and Poetics", 1962.
*Taught as a Professor of Han-Ra Univ..
*Taught as a Inviting Professor of Keonggi Univ..
*Representative Prof. of 'Gwangju Literary Art Collete'.
*Served as a Chairman of 'the Gwangju Forum', Geonggido.
* President of the World Poetry
*A Member of the Literary Men's Association of Korea.
*A Director of Freedom Poets Association of Korea.
*A Central Committee of the Modern Literary Association.
*Won the 'Great' Prize from "the Literary Movement & Trend ", (1998).
*Won the 'Original' Prize from the Freedom Poets Association, (2000).
*Poetic Anthology: <The Weight of Longing>, <The Silence of Wind>, <The Flower and The Wind>, <Drawing a Sound of Light>, <Living As What I am>, <Repetition of Longing and Love>, <The Wave of Nature and Universe>, <A Vortex of my Life>, and <The By-Road of My Life>.

The heaven is lowering.
The healthy man has to sham death,
Because he seems to take our spirit back.

The rolling raindrops on pumpkin leaves near my ears,
From the behind shape
Of their breathing, their gesture driving them gaspingly,
Someone calling makes me stroll idly.

I am waiting to face something.
Meeting and separating,
The time and tide I rule over plainly in my own way,
Is the prepared share.

- Tr. by Won Eung-soon

오늘 그리고 내일

아무리 살아도 알 수가 없다
저승 가까이 쏘다니며
산다는 거
그게 어디 쉬운 일인가.

여름내 바람 뒤채이며
대궁에 매달려 죽음을 부추긴다
아우성 가득 담긴 함정 속에서 마다
앞 못 보고 사는 오늘이어도
문을 열어 나를 가두고 싶다

하늘이 낮아지고 있다
성한 사람 죽은 시늉이라도
혼을 되찾을 수 있을 것 같기 때문이다.

귓속엔 호박 잎새에 구르는 빗방울들
숨차게 몰아가는 숨결, 몸짓
그 뒷모습에서
누군가의 부름이 나를 바장이게 한다.

무언가 맞으려 기다리고 있다
만나고 헤어지면서
분명히 나대로 다스리는 세월
마련된 몫이다.

The Cry of Nature *1)

- An Agricultural Manners of Life-

Birds cry at dawn
Getting up to beg for feed.*2)

Wild cats are crying
Because of no rat to catch, feeling hungry.

The scarecrows that farmers set up pulling ropes,
Out cries of shooing birds away disappeared in history,
Sparrows passing the night in the open air.
Are chirping with tweets for being afraid of night.

The cries of ecosystem yearning after the green aroma,
The cries of nature.

- Tr. by Won Eung-soon

Note:
*1) This poem won the great prize at the 2nd Modern Literary Trend (Monthly Magazine).
*2) It means bird's feed. Cats eat stock feed.

Eun Hee-tae/ Korea

*Pen Name: Seokcheon.
*Poet & Essayist.
*Director of Jeoneup Branch, Literary Mens' Association of Korea.
*Adviser of the Rural Literary Association(4th, 5th, Ex-director)
*Received the 3rd Prize of the Rural Literature, the 11th Prize of Seopo Literature, and won the great prize for Public Subscription of Modern Literary Trend.
*Poetic Anthologies: Maple's Pictures in Mind of Late Autumn; The Cry of Nature, etc.

자연의 울음소리*[1)]

- 農村風俗圖 -

먼동이 트면 새가 운다
일어나 모이 달라고*[2)]

들고양이 울고 있다
이제 잡을 쥐도 없고 배고프다고

허수아비 세우고 줄 당기며
새 쫓는 우여~소리 역사 속으로
초가집 둥지 잃은 노숙자 참새들
찍찍 밤이 두려워 울고 운다.

녹향 그리운 생태계 울음소리
자연의 울음소리

* 1) 제 2회 현대문학사조 현상공모 대상작품
2) 새들의 먹이 곡물, 고양이는 사료를 주고 있음.

The Sunwoon Temple

Around the way to the Sunwoon Temple
The tree's barks sits in the flowers.
The setting sun where the leaves of tree fall on the flower's petal,
And their gestures that they refuse shivering with a fear
Display a grand landscape engraved whitely,
Which the greenness swells up so as to be rent.

With the trees, at the entrance of the valley
Which they look at departing from this world,
The place to rest, clear air, and the wind-bell's sound,
Only I am embraced in the nature's wide bosom now, and
Forget the red setting sun instantly with a vacant mind.

The Buddha's hall of a splendid mural
With long lattice windows flower-patterned, cleanses my weak mind
Full of avarice and vanity like winds.

Eun Yo-suk/Korea

* Completed the Dept of National Language and Literature in the Air and Correspondence College, Korea.
* Recommended as a Poet in Globe Literature.
* Served as Vice President of Baek-Ya Literary Institute.
* A Member of Literary Man's Association of Korea.
* Vice President of the World Poetry Research Institute.
* A Member of Editorial Staff in Traffic & Environment Newspaper.
* Poetical Anthology: "The Snail's Dream".
* Address: 1638-5, Sinlim Bon-Dong, Gwanak-gu, Seoul,151-029, Korea.

The folding screen, encircled behind the main building of the temple,
Its attached hall, and the camellias blooming fully like snow flakes,
Says to us "open your eyes toward the world",
If this is an unseen virtual image, making pretty clothes.

While I was passing over the souls of trees
I knew first in the valley of the Sunwoon Temple
That its sound of wood block made my heart throb.

- Tr. by Won Eung-soon

선운사

선운사 가는 길은
나무의 껍질들이 꽃 속에 앉아 있다
나뭇잎이 꽃잎에 떨어지는 석양
파르르 떨며 거부하는 몸짓은
녹색이 터질 듯 부풀어 오르는
하얗게 음각된 원대한 풍경이다

이 세상 떠나는 것을 바라보는
계곡 입구의 나무들
쉴 자리와 맑은 공기 그리고 풍경 소리
나도 이제는 가슴이 넓은
자연의 품에 안겨 있을 뿐
허탈하게 물든 노을을 잠시 잊는다

꽃살 분합문 화려한 벽화의 법당
탐욕과 허영으로 가득 찬
나약한 마음 바람처럼 씻어주고
대웅전과 영산전 뒤로 두른 병풍
눈송이처럼 후루루 피어나는 동백꽃
보이지 않는 허상이라면 곱게 옷 지어
세상의 눈을 뜨라고 한다

나무들의 영혼을 지나가는 동안
목탁 소리가 가슴을 설레게 하는 것도
선운사 계곡에서 처음 알았다

On Death

___ at evening,

Farmers sowed seeds and the red sea that the young men bled
Falling down on the barley hill early evening,
Beyond there the crows flied about the sky.

Came in flocks, crows,
Pecking at their flesh deeply, deeply,
Washing bones in pieces by dews,
The long cries flowing out like this snakes
Covered the hill lying the other way round,

With the moonlight over the summit, for a long time
The crows wept with abandon, keeping with Caw! Caw!
The traders in market were chained to the place.

- Tr. by Won Eung-soon

Gwon O-un/ Korea

* Born at Gangnyung, Gangwon-do, Korea.
* Graduated from Dept. of Literary Art for Creative Product. Seorabeol Arts Univ.
* Taught at Jungang Univ. as An Additional Professor.
*Won the new Poet's Prize of the Poetic Part in Chosun News Paper, 1966.
* Served as a Chief Editor of the Monthly "Hakwon", and as an Editorial Staff and Head of Publication in K.B.S.
* Poetic Anthology: 'Sending a Letter to Governor'. Essay's Collection: 'Now What Will We Long For?'
* Book for Our Language: The Wrong Used 1234 Words, etc.
*Address: 1105-501, Tanhyun-maeul 11 danji, Ilsan-Seo-ku, Goyang City, Kyeonggido, Korea

절명사(絶命詞)

— 저녁 때

씨 뿌리고 壯丁들은 피를 뿌리며
보리밭 언덕에 쓰러지던 초저녁 벌건 바다
저쪽에서 까마귀가 날았다.

구름처럼 몰리었다. 까마귀는
깊이 깊이 입을 댄
우리 조각 뼈 속 닦은 이슬
쓰러져 번득이는 온몸의 빈 곳에서
실뱀처럼 흘러나온 기나긴 울음이
꾸부려 돌아누운 언덕을 쓸며

마루턱에는 달빛이 오래도록
까욱 까욱 까욱 목을 놓고
허옇게 장꾼들은 떠나지 않았다.

The River Streams

Spring Summer Autumn Winter

Winter Autumn Summer Spring

Going Coming Going Coming

Serpent slowly is slidding away

Horse is springing up.

Hong Chon-an/Korea

* Acquired B.A. and M.A. on French Literature at Seoul National University, Ph.D. in Literature at Continental University. Former Ambassador to the Republic of Zaire, Republic of Congo, Republic of Brundi and Republic of Rwanda, Dean of National Unification Institute. President of Literary coterie "Roots".
* A member of P.E.N., Korea Modern Poetry Association.
* Address: 118-2106, Dong-A Cheongsol Apt, Chang-4dong, Dobong-gu, Seoul, Korea
(Tel) 02-902-4038 (H.P) 010-8447-4038

강물은 흐르고

봄 여름 가을 겨울
겨울 가을 여름 봄
가고 오고 가고 오고
오고 가고 오고 가고
뱀이 스르르 지나가고
말이 뛰어 달려온다.

Misjudgment

After they say innocent,
The persons, going to the jail...
Politicians and enterprisers...
The persons, living in illusion,
Mistaking the afformative things for the negative ones,
The negative things for the afformative ones,
And the people are utterly exhausted
In political strife in mud,
So they are mistaken,
Confusing whose answers are right or false.
Also you and I insist only our own voices,
We, not listening to others.
Before blaming upon other's mistakes,
Because we feel difficult,
Whether I live in misjudgment or not,
Look back on yourselves first of all.

- Tr. by Won Eung-soon

Hong Chun-pyo/Korea

Ph.D.of Public Administration
Poet, Essayist, Children's Write
Director of the Korean Writers' Association
Member of the Korean Pen Club of International Pen Club
1st Vice President of the Guro Pranch of the Korean Writers' Association
Director of Namyang Building
Address: Guro 6dong Namyang Building 401,136-40,Guro-gu

착각(錯覺)

깨끗하다고 말한 후
영창가는 사람들……
정치인들 기업인들……
솔직하게 말하는 사람 없어
긍정적인 것을 부정적으로
부정적인 것을 긍정적으로
착각 속에 사는 사람들
이전투구 식 정치싸움에
국민들은 지치고 지쳐
누구의 말이 옳은지
헷갈려 착각하네
너도나도 제 목소리만
남의 말 안 듣는 사람들
올바른 판단 어려워
누구의 잘못 탓하기 전에
나도 착각 속에 사는지
자신부터 뒤돌아 보아라.

Going to the Miraculous Swamp Land

The swamp has the endless road,
And lots of modes of life is wriggling in it.
The far Brazil and Africa, Bangladesh, India,
And Woopo at Changnyung in Korea as the ecological areas
Are reserved as the miraculous swamp land.
The famished emperor in the forest is the otter,
Not only animals, but also plants
Are protected to be reserved together with their lives,
The wild animals in land are called the lions, the tigers, and hyenas.
But the otters as emperor in water are living on fishes more than flesh and meat,
Drying their bodies in the sun
Thinking proudly this swamp as their basic ground,
They also flow upstream, flowing freely

Hong Yun-pyeo/Korea

* Poet, Sijo(A Tree-Verse Korean poem) poet
* Born in Dang-jin, Chung-nam, in 1950
* Graduated from Korea Open Univ., Kyong-hee Univ., Graduated from graduated school of Gong-joo (public administration M.A.,)
* Awarded Budding Writer through the literary magazine "Farmer", "Literary World", and recommended as a poet by "sijo
* Published Poetical books such as "Spending Winter", A Crane Village", "Like A Wind and Dew", To Bloom A Crane Village", The Flower of Salt", "Dreaming Grand Bridge of West Sea", Published Sijo poetical work "An Azalea in Ami Mountain"
* Wrote the words for the song such as "Spring in An-kook Temple", "My Love Firefly"(International Record: A Song in My Mind)
* Member of International Pen Club in Korea Headquarters, Korea Writer's Association, Korea poetry Association", "Korea Music Copyright Association" Korea Sijo(Korean style poem) Literary Association", "kyung-Hee Writer's Association"
* The present Dang-jin branch manager of Korea writer's Association
* Address: (Nuskin Dangin Center) 238-1, Eupnae-dong, Dangjin-si, Chung-nam, Korea.
Tel: 041-355-3844, Cell No: 010-7434-3844

Along the water course to be a kind with the sea
Sometimes they move busily to save the ecosystem,
Making their houses as building with mud,
While the sand crabs pitch a big camp using mud as a shield
Drinking the high tide and low one
In order to control basic salt,
And they let us know how heathy the swamp is keeping.

- Tr. by Won Eung-soon

기적의 습지를 가다

습지는 끝없는 길이 있다
기적의 습지에는 생태가 꿈틀거린다
기적의 생태는 저 멀리 브라질 아프리카
방글라데시 인도 창녕우포늪이
기적의 습지로 보호되고 있다
동물을 보호하고
식물을 보호하며 생을 이어가는 습지
허기진 물속의 황제는 수달이다
육지의 맹수는 호랑이 사자 하이네가
성(城)을 이루고 있지만
수달은 물속의 황제라고 육류보다는 물고기로
명을 이어가며 햇살에 몸을 말린다
습지는 나의 삶터라 자랑스럽게
물줄기 굽이굽이 역류하고 완만하게 흐르고 흘러
바다가 이웃이며 동족이다
때론 수중에 기적의 생태를 구하여
자연을 살리며 자연에 빌딩처럼
집을 짓고, 진흙을 옷 삼아
농아자인 농게들은 붉게 진을 친다
오르내리는 밀물과 썰물을 마시며
때론 염도를 낮추며 기적의 습지에
고도를 낮춰 안부를 묻는다.

Nude Croquis

Three minutes bloomed fully
Near, the more nearly the silent smile
Drawn for the lack of expression, our eyes move up and down the naked body.

Though a slanting black line grazed its white nape,
The model's muscle, excluded feelings is brilliant.
The facial expression of stationery things and hidden curved lines are moved,
The ceased time
Is the line's strong and weak showing only line and line.

For a long and short your
The sweat's stream flowing between the base rock of the burning sand
Shows a mystic canyon hidden in the hip.

Jang Hyun-kyung/Korea

* Born at Yecheon, Gyeongsangbukdo
* Poet, Essayist, Critic, Pen Name: Jajeong.
* Made his Debut as the poem "The Spring Cold with 2 other poems", 2006 and at the same year, issued an essay, "The Little Killing Field".
* Published the poetic Anthology of "When the Apricot Blooms Fully", 2008 and had a party in honor of its publication of the poetic book.
* Set up a Signboard of "Parolho Literary Village", 2008.
* A Member of the Literary Association of Korea.
* A Member of the World Poetry Literary Research Institute of Korea.
* A Chairman of the Cheonggye Literary Society.
* Won the Prize of Mul-Rye Literature, of the World Poetry, of the New Literature, and of Heo-nan-seol-heon Literature.
* Present Address: 40-3, Joongkog 2nd Dong, Gwangjingu, Seoul, Korea.

It is a unfinished flower blooming and falling in an instant
Not exposing, if we don't care of it.

The blank space, being sick with 3 minutes' scarcity,
Discloses untouched distance forever,
It is the gap of time not to get over,
And the prohibited line not to allow the detail's description...

So it's a genre of arts showing a love
To be left behind in a longer trailing than a sharing time together.

- Tr. by Won Eung-soon

누드 크로키

활짝 핀 3분
무표정에 그려지는 은은한 미소
가까이 더 가까이 시선들이 나신을 오르내린다.

검은 색 빗금이 희디흰 목덜미를 스쳐도
감정이 배제된 모델의 근육은 눈부시다.
정물의표정과 숨은 곡선이 옮겨지고
멈춰버린 시간은
라인과 라인만을 보여 주는 선의 강약

길고도 짧은 시간
태양이 작열하는 사막의 암반 사이로 흐르는 땀줄기
엉덩이에 감춰진 신비의 협곡

관심 둬 주지 않으면 나오지 않는
찰나에 피고 지는 미완의 꽃이다.

3분의 결핍을 앓는 여백은
영원히 닿지 않는 거리
넘어서지 못할 세월의 틈새
세부 묘사를 허락하지 않는 골 패인 금지선……

함께한 시간보다 더 긴 여운으로
남의 사랑을 보여 주는 예술 장르.

Confession

Now there are
Marvellously
Wonderful things
In my head.

These marvellously things are---,
When I would like to express them
In words and in writing,
Strangely,
Something grows wrong a little.

In case of 'happiness'
There are much finer happiness
Than the ordinary little one in my head,
The happiness in words, and also the happiness in writing,
So it is, as it has done.

Jeong Ji-ahn/Korea

* Born in A-san city, Choongnam , in 1961
* Graduated from Dongguk Univ., Dept. of Ind. Eng. (BS)
* Graduated from graduate school of Dongguk Univ., Dep. Of Ing. (MS/Ph.D)
* Present: Assistant Professor at Shinsung College
* Address: Rm 207, 103-dong, Hyundai Green Apt., Sigok-ri, Dangjin-eup, Choongnam, 343-753, Korea

In case of ‘love’
There are much higher level’s love
Than the ordinary one in my head,
The love in words, and also the love in writing,
So it is, as it has done.

Haha~, it’s exorbitant, very whacking.
Fortunately,
It’s also lucky
Not to express them.

- Tr. by Won Eung-soon

고백

지금 머릿속에는
엄청나게
멋있는 것들이
들어 있습니다.

이 엄청난 것들이 말이예요
말과 글로
나타내려고 하면
이상하게도
뭔가 조금씩 틀어져 버립니다.

행복도
그냥 일상의 소소한 행복보다
훨씬 더 대단한 행복이 머릿속에 있는데
말로도 행복, 글로도 행복
그냥 이렇게만 됩니다.

사랑도
그냥 보통 사랑보다
훨씬 높은 수준의 사랑이 머릿속에 있는데
말로도 사랑, 글로도 사랑
그냥 이렇게만 됩니다.

하~ 엄청납니다, 엄청나
다행이
표현할 수 없어서
또한 다행입니다.

A Story of the Sumjin River

The more secluded late autumn of the Sumjin river
Meanders at the end of the great Taebaek Mountain
Winding and caressing a sad ground.

It embraces the ripped body of salmons
Rising against the river in order to spawn,
And keeps step with the crabs for returning to sea
Tickling the riverside in their slow steps.
How is their life so sad a desperate fight?
The late autumn evening, receiving their end
That they couldn't get over their destiny,
Is lonesome.

Even being scratched by poor fisherman's netting,
The mother river, giving out all herself,
Getting the best of death, conceiving new lives,
And existing the best abundantly,
But herself was always lonesome mother river.

Jeong Ji-won / Korea

* Pen Name: Seo Woo
* Born in Jeonju, 1970.
* Made her Debut as a Poet in "the Literary Trend" monthly.
* Reciting Poet(Won the Great Prize of National Reading Meeting0
* A Member of World Poetry Literature & of Baek-Ya Literary Society.

Standing at the Sumjin riverside at late autumn,
The river tells me in her own deep voice,
A certain sad fisherman's story,
Which the salmons spawn in order to die, rising against the river,
The crabs also spawn in order to die, returning to sea.

- Tr. by Won Eung-soon

섬진강 이야기

굽이치는 대간(大幹)의 끝자락
설움의 땅을 휘감고 다독이며 흘러 돌아
더욱 그윽해진 늦가을의 섬진강

산란을 위해 강을 거슬러 오르는
연어들의 찢긴 몸을 젖가슴 열어 안고
느린 옆걸음으로 강기슭을 간질이며
바다로 회유하는 참게들을 떠밀며 발을 맞춘다
목숨이 이렇게도 처연한 사투일까
끝내 숙명을 타넘지 못한
어족(漁族)들의 최후를 거두는
섬진강의 늦가을 저녁은 쓸쓸하다

가난한 어부의 그물질에 할퀴어지면서도
바닥까지 긁어 내어주는 어머니 강
죽음을 이기고 새 생명을 잉태하는,
가장 풍성히 존재하되,
그 스스로는 늘 외로운 모천(母天)

늦가을 섬진강가에 서면
강은 예의 그 깊은 목소리로
어느 슬픈 어족의 이야기를 들려준다
연어는 알을 낳고 죽기 위해 강을 거스르고
참게는 알을 낳고 죽기 위해 바다로 간다고......

For You

My star smaller than dust
In the small star, an earth
Of uncountable planets shining in the heaven,
Met you, was a mysterious fortune.

When I look at your clear eyes like a fountain,
New vision gushed forth,
Your check like a peach blossom
Was as warm as spring of home.

On the day, driving dark crowds
From the clear blue sky, as I don't forsee,
We wish to look at the only bright future
Under the brilliant shining sun.

While I am staying for a little while in the world,
I will share the warm heart with you,
Fill up your love in my heart,
And bloom the lovely karma with you.

- Tr. by Won Eung-soon

Jeong Jin-su/Korea

* Born in Incheon City, Korea.
* Serving at the National Tax Office(Present)
* Graduate from Dept. of National language of the Air and Correspondence College
* Member of the Literary Circle in National Tax Office
* Member of the Association of the Literary Trend and Thought
* Member of the World Poetry Institute
* Won a Literary Prize from the World Poetry Institute

*Address: 4384, Singil 4-dong, Samsung Laemian Apt. 109-301, Youngdeunpo-gu. Seoul, Korea.

그대를 위하여

하늘에 빛나는 수많은 행성 중에
지구라는 작은 별에서
먼지보다 작은 나의 별
그대 만남은 신비로운 행운입니다

샘처럼 맑은 눈동자 바라보면
새로운 희망이 솟아오르고
복숭아꽃 같은 그대 볼은
고향의 봄처럼 따뜻하였습니다

마른 하늘에 검은 먹구름장
몰려오는 날, 예측할 순 없지만
찬란한 태양이 빛나는
밝은 미래만 바라보고 살면 좋겠습니다

지상에 잠시 머무르는 동안
따뜻한 마음 나누고
가슴속에 사랑 가득 채워서
그대와 아름다운 인연을 꽃 피우렵니다

A Long Letter of a Crane

Snow falls silently,
Snow falls blankly.
On the mountains and rivers at sundown,
The cranes come down on the withered trees,
Leave posthumous records
Instead of the notes, dancing.

At the long sundown,
After turning the alarm clock's needle round,
The smoke of the backwoods
As expecting the departed son,
Is writing a long letter in the waste land,
Whirling the foamy river.

- Tr. by Won Eung-soon

Jin Sang-soon / Korea

*Ex-Chairman of Writer's Association at Gimjae Branch
*President at General Society of Arts of Korean Painting
*Member of Literary Men's Association of Korea
*Vice Chairman of Kirin Literature at Jeon-Buk
*Member of Literary Men's Association of Jeon-Buk
*A Compilation Committee of A Dictionary of Modern Poets in Korea
*Received Prizes:
- Chosen Four Times at The Nation-Wide Arts Exhibition of Byok-Gol
- Won the Prize of new Poet from "The Han-Kook Poetry" monthly
- Won the Great Prize from "The Han-Kook Poetry" monthly
- Won the Prize of Culture of Gimjae Citizens
- Won the Prize of Nosan Literature
*Publication:
- An Extra Star, Hanging in the Sky, The Reason the Wind Sits on the Tree, Now and Then, On Such A Day, Long Letters of A Crane

학의 장서

고요히 눈이 내린다
하염없이 눈이 내린다
해저녁 산수강산에
학춤이 내려앉아
고사목 대신장부에
유고의 기록을 남긴다

석양이 늘어질 때
자명종을 돌려놓고
떠난 자식 바라보는
두메산골 저녁연기
거품 문 강을 휘돌아
광야에 장서를 쓴다.

South and North

The children of South and North of Korea
Are pulling an elastic string hard each other,
Which somebody gave it to them.

Without inquiring who, when, and why it has done,
If they by chance fail to catch the string,
The pulling side children are afraid of hurting their faces.

The children of South and North,
For fear of future troubles,
Are pulling an elastic cord hard each other.

How long will they pull it only?
The adults who gave it drew back
To be onlookers,

Whether we only look at the dangerous conducts
Against our conscience, or not,
What a great sadness of South and North of Korea it is!

- Tr. by Won Eung-soon

Jun Duk-ki/Korea

* A Member of the Literary Men's Association of Korea.
* A Director of the International Pen Club in Korea Headquarter.
* A Director of the Modern Poets Association.
* Poetical Anthology: <The Grassland without Dew> with other 10 vols.
* A Collection of Column: <Open Mind, the Blue Heart> with other 4 vols.
* A Collection of Essay: <Silvery Sands of My Life I Picked Up While Working> with other 2vols.
*The Selected Poems: <The Road to that Land> with other 3 vols.
* Address: 147, Dongsomundong 4ga, Seongbukgu, Seoul, Korea.

남과 북

남과 북의 아이들은
누군가가 쥐어준 고무줄을
서로 열심히 당기고만 있다

누가 언제 왜 따질 겨를도 없이
행여 놓칠세라 놓치면
열심히 당기던 쪽이 얼굴을 상하기에

남과 북의 아이들은
후환이 두려워
서로 열심히 고무줄을 당기고만 있다

어느 때까지 당기기만 할 것인가
쥐어준 어른들은 뒤로 물러나
구경꾼이 되었으니

이 위험한 양심 없는 행위를
언제까지 보고만 있을 것인지
남과 북의 애통함이여!

The Melody of Blue Mountain

I drink Blue Mountain,
Its sweet rhythm staying in my mouth,
And its fragrance vibrating like Cello's melody,
That is *' Adagio in G-minor'.

For appeasing the victims' sadness
Sacrificed at the internal war of Bosnia,
The most beautiful musical performance of peace
Opened with not powerful, but touching heart deeply.

I drink its sadness with a cup of tea.
Their surviving days for existence was always a strained life.
I reflect on my days that have quarreled with others without reasons,
Because of the unforgettable events.

In the night when the silent melody fills the room,
And when it is a memory, or a yearning,
Or even a low happiness,
Even though drinking several cups of coffee a day,
I drink the different kinds of coffee from they are,
Today I love to drink a cup of coffee with a justifiable reason.

- Tr. by Won Eung-soon

* Albinony, Adagio G-minor: At that time, 1992, in Bosnia Internal war, its capital city was Sarajevo, and 22 good citizens were killed by the dropped bomb. A Cellist played the above melody beside that place.

Jun Min-Jeong/Korea

* Recommended as a New Poet from the Monthly Monthly Magazine of ChangJo-Munye
* Member of Public Information of the Korean Writers`
* Vice Secretary General of the Korea Christian Poets` Association
* Director of Litetary Association of Recitation for Korean Poetry
* Poetical Anthology : How Can We Compare You with the Flower?
* Receiving Prize : Won a great Prize of the Korea Cultural Environment(Poetry Section)

블루마운틴의 선율

불루마운틴을 마신다
입안에 머무는 감미로운 운율
첼로의 선율처럼 떨리는 향내
'아다지오 G단조'

보스니아 내전 파편에
희생된 이들의 슬픔을 위해
세상에서 가장 아름다운 평화의 연주
강하지도 않으면서 가슴을 울리는 것

차 한 잔을 마시며 슬픔도 함께 마신다
살아온 날들은 팽팽한 긴장의 연속이었구나
까닭도 없이 다투었던 나를 돌아다본다
잊을 수 없는 그 무엇들로

고요한 선율이 방안 가득 깔리는 밤
기억일 때도 그리움일 때도
그저 느슨한 행복일 때도
하루에 몇 잔씩 커피를 마셔도
단 한 잔도 똑같지 않았던 커피
난 오늘도 이유 있는 커피를 마신다

* 알비노니 '아다지오 G단조' : 1992년 보스니아 내전 당시 수도 사라예보는 전쟁터, 포탄이 떨어져 무고한 시민 22명이 죽자 한 첼리스트가 포탄이 떨어졌던 장소 바로 옆에 자리를 잡고 연주를 시작했다.

A Road of Autumn

The time makes a trip silently
With the cicada's chirrup,
And it's bringing autumn with a cricket's chirp slowly.

The red dragonfly longs so its old retrospect
As to dance flying in the space,
The voice of over the footpath between rice ridges
Is being heard as the delight news of a harvest.

Will I be matured too?
A part of my soul turns red
With the laps of time to come near.

- Tr. by Won Eung-soon

Jung Sun-ja / Korea

* Pen Name: So-Yeun.
* Born at Soondheon, Jeon-Nam, Korea.
* Graduated from the Course of the Graduate School of Administration in Ewha Woman's University.
* Served as a Chairman of the Essay Literature of Ewha Woman's Univ., its Counselor(Present).
* A Member of the Literary Men's Association of Korea, International Pen Club, and a Director of Recommendation of Essayist Committee.
* Received the Prize of "the Jang-Han Mother", the Prize of Minister of Physical Bureau of '88 Seoul Olympic Game, of the Literary Art of Soondheon Girls' High School, and of Essay Part of 'the Huh Nan Seul Heon' Art.
* Essay Anthology: "Tolling at a Mountain Temple", with other 2 Vols.
* Address: 247-162, Seokyodong, Mapogu, Seoul, Korea.

가을이 오는 길

긴 여름 매미 소리 따라
살며시 여행 떠나고
귀뚜라미 소리 천천히 손잡고
가을을 데려 오고 있구려

고추잠자리 옛 추억 그리워
허공을 나는 춤사위
논두렁 너머 곡식 여무는 소리
수확의 기쁜 소식 들려오는데

나도 성숙해가는 것인가
영혼의 한 자락이 다가오는
세월 따라 단풍이 든다

A Dandelion

The white dandelion, though anyone doesn't gaze with deep
interest,
Blooming silently without being broken off by hardships,

Like the deeper mother's bosom,
Its noble, hot passion
Bloomed with silimarin and cholin ingredients
Preserving its sweet ,bitter, and salty taste.

It strengthens our internal organs
As in its cold function, getting worse in drinking a few cups
With tete-a-tete at the closing hour,
And heals up inflammation and clears up blood,
Governing the soul of our race.

- Tr. by Won Eung-soon

Kang Young-duk/Korea

* Start a literary career through monthly magazine 'Munhak 21' in 1998
* Put my name on a biographical dictionary in 2002
* Put my literary work on the biographical encyclopedia
* A member of "SGI literary man's association" "the world poet research institute" "kangnam literary man's club" "guro literary man's club" "millennium literary man's association"
* Joint literary work: A Clamor, A String of leaves, Yearning becomes flower by the expression in your eyes, The Wind that Bring Life

* Address: 1-202, Daehan apt., 381-18, Hwagok7-dong, Gangseo-gu, Seoul, 157-885. Korea
* E-mail: luxvia @yahoo.co.kr * Phone NO: 02-2604-8234/ 010-9970-8234

민들레

봐 주는 이 딱히 없어도
풍설에 꺾임 없이 묵묵히 피어나는

동서양이 판치는 들녘의 여기저기에서도
도심의 시멘트 아파트 벽 틈에서도
자존심을 지켜가는 하얀 민들레

깊고 깊은 어머니 품처럼
고귀한 뜨거운 열정은
실리마린과 콜린성분으로 피어나
쓰고 달고 짠맛의 오묘함을 담아

한잔 두잔 나누는 퇴근길 정담 속에
약화되어 가는 오장육부 기능을
차가운 성질로 이로움을 평정하여
염증을 없애고 피를 맑게 하며
민족의 얼을 품고 다스려 주고 있구나

Two Days at the Gangchon Village

Go to the green colored Gangchon **yeowul-neowul*
With our hands and legs spreading out forward **joog-joog*,
Breading the grass's aroma **hoo-hoo* as much as we like,
With knapsacks on our shoulders stepping out *sambak-sabak lightly.

At a lane walking together **soall-poall* with a breeze,
We meet you **ulssa*, who have missed for a long time,
You meet me **doong-doong*, after looking for,
At a lane the moon is ripening **sarak-morak* fully.

Let go to the mountain and river **sallang-challang* in Gangchon,
With the lane spent over the night of stars **sokeun-sakeun*,
Someone asking, how are you harmonized in a line of longitude and latitude.,
Say to him, two days at the Gangchon village.

- Tr. by Won Eung-soon

* The italicized adjectives words are all special, interesting modifying Korean vocabularies.

Kim A-lang/Korea

*Published poetical works titled 'Adrg Leaf on the Earth', 'A plain', 'A gaze at a Thorny Bush',
* An auditor of Seongdo literary circles, a curator of Harvard school, a teacher at yeongje nursery
* A member of the blue sky club of an air force, member of the Korea Writer Association, member of farmer's literature club, and so on
* Address: 102-806, Chunggu Apt, shinbanpo, jamwondong, seochogu, Seoul, Korea
* E-mail: alangk@hanmail.net * Tel: 010-7470-4936

강촌에서의 이틀

초록빛 여울너울 강촌에 가자
팔다리 쭉-쭉 어깨를 펴고
풀내음 후-후 들이마시며
발걸음 삼박사박 배낭을 매고

솔바람 소올포올 함께 가는 길
잃었던 얼-싸 널 만나고
헤매던 둥-둥 날 만나서
달빛이 사락모락 익어가는 길

산과 물 살랑찰랑 강촌에 가자
별들이 소근새근 밤을 새던 길
어떻게 날줄씨줄 어우러졌냐
물으면 강촌에서의 이틀이라고

Dreaming the Eden Garden

In front of the gutter of the central city
Spitting the gravy of three-ply pork,
I have vomited feeling sick.

Under a catchword
Even drawing a water-colour of the Han river,
We cannot take care of the drainage vent.

Singing the green woods and clear water,
If we have a dreaming conscience,
And think a little deeply

About our pretty lips and anus,
We should treat them on the same footing,
Before our realities of life different from the inside and the outside,

Suddenly, the life of Eden Garden with nothing on
Flashed across my mind.

- Tr. by Won Eung-soon

Kim Baek-kyeong/ Korea

* Pen Name: Bobae * Born in Goheung, Jeon-nam.
* Recommended as a poet in 'Munyechunchoo'.
* Issued such Collaborated Anthologies as 'The Haedong Literature', 'The Sinmunye', 'The Munhaksegye' and The Literary Movement & Trend, etc.
* Won the prize of 'International Culture and Art', of 'the Manree Literature', of 'the Hurnansulhan Literature.
- Present: * Member of Literary Writer's Association.
* Manager of Cultural Exchange of Overseas in Korea.
* Official Director of Underwater Environmental Association.
* Official Director of the Arrangement Committee for foundation of the Cultural Art of Dokdo Island

에덴을 꿈꾸다

삼겹살 육수를 토하는
도심의 하수구 앞에서
구역질이 나고야 말았다

말로는
한강의 수채화를 그리면서
수챗구멍하나 간수 못 하는구나

푸른 숲과 맑은 물을 노래하며
꿈꾸는 양심이라면
예쁜 입술과 냄새나는 항문

조금만 깊이 생각하면
똑같이 대우해 주어야만 하는 것을
겉과 속이 다른 우리들의 현실 앞에서

문득, 발가벗고 살았다던 에덴동산이 떠오른다.

The Laborer

The sun dawns before the exhausted body is relaxed,
And I go to work without breakfast,
Because of urgent business and of losing appetite.

Having two or three dishes of lunch,
I feel empty even taking a meal again,
Yet am not satiated at all, even taking a meal again.

I cannot go back home with fatigued body through all day,
So drinking wines and what is more, being abused,
How is it poor thing!

Wife's heart breaks torn to pieces,
It keeps wife's heart worried sick all the time.

- Tr. by Won Eung-soon

Kim Bok-nam / Korea

* Completed the whole course of study at Free Literary Univ.
* A member of Jeonbuk Free Poetry
* A chairwoman of the Twenty-fourth Yucho
* A member of a literary group which publishes a magazine "The Sound of a Leaf"
* A member of Baikja Literature
* A member of the World Poetry research Institute
* Address: 101-1205, Dongguk Apt, 1034-1, Jinbuk2-dong, Deogjin-gu, Jeonju-si, Jeon-buk, 561-782, Korea

노동인

지친 몸 풀기 전 해가 밝았네
갈 시간이 급해서 입맛이 없어
아침을 거르고 일하러 가네

점심은 두 그릇 아니면 세 그릇
먹어도 먹어도 눈은 퀭하고
먹어도 먹어도 배 부르지 않네

하루 종일 지친 몸 이대로 귀가 못해
술먹고 욕먹고 불쌍하여라

어서 가서 휴식을 취하고 나서
내일 아침 일하러 가면 좋으련

마누라 간덩이 다 타들어가네
마누라 애간장 다 녹아나네

The Water-colored Peace

In the new morning
When we face the river, its water color is white.
The soaring sun sprinkles its silver pieces.
This side sands and that side ones where I stand on barefoot,
Shine all in white colors.
It's not the blue river, but a white river of naked face.

At the evening twilight
When I see the river, its color is ruddy.
The western sky pours its red pollen down to the river
The waves of western plains and the temple from the river hill
  where I stand
Lap in scarlet colors of its light.
Now it's not the blue river, but a blushed river.

Every moment, it dyes in the water-colored peace, truly.

- Tr. by Won Eung-soon

Kim Chong-ki/Korea

* Born in Sun Cheon city(1938~)
* Graduated from Goryou Universty majoring on Korean Literature, pre-principal of Suong Eui Girls High School Korean Literature, presbyter of Korean Presbyterian Church, made a debut as a poet by 'Christian Literature' 'Trend of Literature' 'Modern Sijo'
* Member of Korean Literature Association, member of International PEN Club in Korean Branch, awarded by Young Rang Literature Prize, Christian Poet Prize, Trend of Literature Prize and Epipodo Literature Prize
* Collections: As Sunrays in Vacant site (1991), Laugh Bunged up on End of Nose, Sorrow Always Living in My Mind, I'll Live Unreservedly and Gay-spiritedly, A star Alive in My Mind literary group magazine : High Jump Of Grasshopper, The clean person washing even though the tear
*Address: 621, Sanghadong, Giheunggu, Yongin City, Suwon-dongmaeul Ssangyong Apt. 303-1701, Geonggido, Korea.

물빛의 평화

새 아침에
강을 마주하면 물빛이 하얗다.
솟는 햇빛이 은(銀) 조각을 뿌리고 있다.
내가 발 벗고 서 있는 이쪽의 모래밭과
저 건너 모래밭까지 은색으로 반짝인다.
푸른 강이 아니라 흰 민낯의 강이다.

저녁노을에
강을 보면 물빛이 불그레하다.
서천이 강으로 붉은 꽃가루를 쏟는다.
내가 서 있는 강 언덕에서 서쪽 들판과
가람의 물결이 분홍 빛보라로 찰랑댄다.
푸른 강이 아니라 낯붉힌 강이다.

시시각각 물드는 물빛의 평화, 진솔하다.

Dokdo Island

Here
All things turn into rocks,
Nay, mystic ones,
Unable to leave more, or
To budge an inch,
Making a lump of serious loneliness.

In the face of strong winds and waves,
The grasses, the trees, the birds, and the flowers
Turn into great rocks of loneliness,
Converging the still breaths of fifty millions of people.

Here
Upon the great sea
Waving billows in the blue sea,
Dokdo opens dawn earlier
In blue color of 5 thousand years
Towers high as a lonesome rock
Having endured for countless years.

O,
Dokdo, Dokdo island!
The invincible figure, be forever,
Dokdo, engraved with the spirit of Korean people...

Kim Don-young/Korea

* Pen Name: Eunro. Born at Youngkwang, Jeonnam, Korea.
* Graduated from the Air and Correspondence College.
* First Debut as a Poet through "the Sinchoon Literary Arts" and "Literary Movement & Trend". * A Photo-Writer(Present).
*A Member of Literary Writer's Association of Korea.
* Poetic Anthology: "The Wind's Whisper"
* Address: 311-13, Bulkwangdong, Metrotower 2206, Eunpyunggu, Seoul Korea.

독도

여기서는
모두 돌이 된다
더는, 떠날 수도,
오갈 수도 없는
독한 외로움으로 뭉쳐
신비한 돌이 된다.

거센 바람 파도에 굴하지 않고
풀과 나무와 새와 꽃
오천만의 잔잔한 숨결 모아
그리움의 큰 돌이 된다.

여기
푸른 물결 넘실대는
큰 바다 위에
오천년의 하늘빛으로
앞서 앞서서 새벽을 열고
억겁의 세월 견뎌온
고독한 바위로 우뚝 섰다.

오,
독도여!
불굴의 자태 영원하리
대한민족의 얼이 새겨진 독도여...

Song for A Single-Heartedness of Chunhyang

A destiny, tied with her back feeling a chill !
Rubbing her hands, and feeling her heart torn to pieces,
She draws a blue picture on her clear white face.

Her confession, engraved in a jade ring!
Eternal promises, opened her heart passionately
Are an unbroken fate even if snapped her body.

Though a sword threatens her in the terrible command,
Her single-heartedness, tied with heaven's will, for sweet heart,
Nothing in the world can break her true mind.

Trembling, desiring, she makes angry waves calm down,
And coming across *O-jak Bridge facing against rainstorm,
She enjoys a festival with her lover under the nettle trees.

- Tr. by Won Eung-soon

* O-jak Bridge: it means a legendary bridge which crows and magpies form in order to meet lovers on the day of 7th July in old calender.

Kim Eui-shik/Korea

* Born in Sangju,Gyeongbuk. Grown up Chungju *Pen-name: Cheong-seok * Now serves concurrently as a professor at Inha University
* A Visiting Professor at Incheon University
* A lecturer at the Juvenile financial education centre
* A director at Save zone I&C * A director of Institute of managing the Global Green(present)* A director at Korea Production Society
* Started a literary career through Literary Movement & Trend
* Published poetical works entitled 'Becoming a root of a dandelion
* Literary work entitled 'Pull an Oar When the Wind Goes Down', Live a wealthy man till Die', Hold the World in Your Bosom' and ten others.
*Address: 328-7, Gildong 2nd-dong, Gangdonggu, Hanmaeum-Jutaek 401, Seoul, Korea.
* Caf adrees : Caf.daum.net/YesKim

춘향의 단심가

등짝을 오싹이며 맺어진 인연이여
손가락 부비면서 간장을 졸여대며
티 없는 하얀 얼굴에 파란 그림 그린다

옥지환(玉指環) 고리 속에 새겨둔 고백이여
뜨겁게 열어 제친 천년의 약속들이
알몸이 잘린다 해도 끊지 못할 운명을!

시퍼런 호령 속에 단검을 든다 해도
하늘에 잡아매 둔 님 향한 일편단심
천지의 기를 모아도 그대만은 못말려

떨면서 갈구면서 성난 물결 재우고
비바람 맞으면서 오작교 건너와서
팽나무 그늘 아래서 축제 마당 벌인다.

The Winter with Leeds

It murmurs around the riverside together,
Plainly that is not only the wind's traces,
Getting away out of the tributary river.
With my blue veins jutting out,
My ears are very keen,
So they are reacting on the sound within me.
I move my toe's end busily dipped in the swamp.
To scoop up from the dried body
Is not water, but life.
It sucks the smell of sunlight and wind
At every fluff sprouted from the dried leaves.
And rubbing the dried stems,
To pile up with one another.
The winter, pausing for breath,
In no time at all calls spring season,
Rubbing their frozen feet under the frozen ground.
The passing migratory birds sat to rest for a moment.
Taking a few warm steam of breath in their mouths,
They fly up toward the snowing sky.

- Tr. by Won Eung-soon

Kim Gui-rye/Korea

* Started a literary career through 'Literary Movement & Trend'
* Majored in Korean Language and Literature at Jeonnam University
* A announcer at MBC(Busan, Gwangju)
* A director of the gathering of woman(Gwangju Branch)
* Completed the course of a speech guidance teacher at Ewha woman University(Educational center), completed the course of an essay-philosophy at Ewha woman University (Educational center)
* A speech consultant, an essay teacher, completed the course of Free Literature University (with the class of 25th)
* President of a literary group 'Majungmul', A member of Jeonbuk free poetry recitation, A director of World Poetry Research Institute

갈대의 겨울

강변이 두런댄다
분명 샛강을 빠져나가는 바람의
흔적만은 아니다
푸른 핏줄이 빠져나가
귀가 예민해진 탓에
내 안에서 나는 소리에 반응하고 있다
늪지에 담근 발가락 끝을 부지런히 꼼질거린다
버석거리는 몸에 내가 퍼 올리는 것은
물이 아니라 생명이다
말려진 잎에 돋은 솜털마다
햇빛 냄새 바람 냄새를 빨아들인다
그리고 마른 줄기를 부비며
서로의 심장을 포갠다
바스러진 껍데기로 한 몸이 되어
숨을 고르는 겨울
어느새 땅속 언 발을 비비며 봄을 부른다
지나던 철새가 잠시 앉았다
따뜻한 입김 몇 장 주워 물고
눈 내리는 하늘로 날아 오른다.

Father's Joy

Two sisters drive their own car.
The younger one drives,
And the older one talks,
"Pig! what you eat?"
"Sundae sausage, oink, oink"
Their laughing voice is heard from father's hand-phone.
"That little pets!"
Father is happy with it.

- Tr. by Won Eung-soon

Kim Hak-jin/Korea

* Born in Gochang
* Be on duty at Asan Hospital in Jheong-up
* Member of the World Poetry Research Institute
* Address: 346, Yonggye-dong, Jeongeup-si, Jeon-buk, 580-230, Korea
Tel: 063-533-9025 / 010-3950-9025

아버지의 기쁨

딸 형제가 승용차를 몰고 간다
동생이 운전을 하고
언니는 지껄인다
돼지야 뭣 먹을래?
순대 꿀꿀
웃는 소리 아버지의 휴대폰에 들린다
고것들!
아버지는 기쁘다.

At a Corner of My Canvas

A handful of the flower's petals infiltrated into a canvas,
Together with the heart
Blooming on the spring's hill of home,
Walking together on the lane of a pear blossom,

They are so mixed one another
Whether they are dyestuff, a floral water, or a maid's heart,
Indulging
Into the indistinguishable palette's fragrance...

Re-coating my heart all over the canvas,
Dyed on the tip of drawing blush,
The past years when we have laughed
In the pink-colored season, or have shed tears
In the grey-colored season are wavering in my eyes..

Kim Hye-sook/ Korea

* Member of Jeonju City Assembly
* Graduated from Granduate School of Jeonju Univ. Ph.D.
* Director of Leadership Center in Female Committee of the Democratic Unified Party
* Vice Chairman of Special Committee of Central
* Environment in Democratic Unified Party
* Served as a Visiting Prof.
* Address: #10 1Gil Nosong Square, Wansan-Gu, Jeonju City Korea
* Mobile : 010-7736-1896
* E-mail : khs-ria@hanmail.net

Never discriminate
Whether the flower's petals, kneaded in the dyestuff
Are the woman's heart,
Traces of the yearning sweetheart !

I lift my hear to the heaven
Indulged in a fuddled state of its fragrance
With my head on a pillow as royal azaleas.

- Tr. by Won Eung-soon

캔버스 일우(一隅)

캔버스에 스며든, 꽃잎 한 송이
복사 꽃길 함께 걷던
고향 봄 언덕 피어나던
마음도 함께 스미어

물감인지. 꽃물인지, 소녀의 마음인지
서로 범벅이 되니
분간 할 수 없는 빠렛트
향기에 젖어드네...

붓끝에 물든 마음
캔버스에 덕지덕지 붙여놓고
분홍빛 시절에 웃고
회색빛 사연에 울던
지난 세월이 아롱지누나......

물감에 이개는 꽃잎이
여인의 마음인지,
그리운 님의 자취인지
구별이 없어라!

혼미한 향취에 젖어
철쭉을 베개 삼아
하늘을 우러른다.

Mountain Doesn't Blame Clouds

Clouds tell us to live like a mountain,
And a mountain does us to live like water.

Clouds flow forward to heaven incessantly.
The mountain goes resting with its standing high.

Clouds hang together to be rain and snow,
And flow looking for the low place, the sea from the mountain.

If clouds does not get out of from darkness,
The mountain confines light, and waits taking a patience.

- Tr. by Won Eung-soon

Kim Hyung-chol/Korea

* Pseudonym: Dong Cho
* Birth place: in BuAn JeonBuk Province
* One of the literary men's Association. Work: But havent been hear a lovable saying
* A eulalia flower of Bong du mound. Prize: Korea poetry great prize
* Address : 351, Bonghwang-ri, Dongjin-Myeon, Buan-gun, Jeon-Buk, Korea

산은 구름을 탓하지 않는다

구름은 산 같이 살라하고
산은 물처럼 살라하네

구름은 천공에 흐르면서 쉼이 없고
산은 우뚝 서 있으나 쉬어가네

구름은 뭉치면 비와 눈이 되어
산에 내려 낮은 곳 찾아 바다로 가네

구름이 어둠 속에 헤어나지 못하면
산은 빛을 가두어 참고 기다리네.

In Hanoi of Vietnam

An array of automobiles and the risky acrobats riding on them,
Like torrents of rain are gathering at the streets of Hanoi
On a drizzle day in the suffocating danger,
Here and there, without previous warning,
So we often think it very surprising, and ruffle tempers,
But Hanoi citizens take such a thing as a matter of course,
Being generous, waiting, and standing aside, without a murmur.
We want to applaud their acts with hands.

After going on a sightseeing tour,
Entering a fine restaurant with a Korean sign to have lunch,
We looked at the menu board translated poorly in Korean,
Only with a broad smile.
The menu said, "O-jing-o-cho-mu-chim[1],
Ye-yak-mong-mun[2], mat-it-neun-pa-jeon.[3]""
We cannot help laughing at it,

Kim Il-rye/Korea

* Born in 1955 in Seung-ju, Jeon-nam
* Graduated from Naju University
* Finished the graduate course of Jeon-nam Univ. (the course of woman leader)
* Finished the training course of Etiquette of Chosun Univ.
* Finished the course of Literary Creation of Kwang-ju Univ.
* Published a collection of essays entitled 'Even the humble has a potential for leadership' in 1996
* Published poetical works entitled 'The fragrance of Lilies' 'You and I are One Flesh' 'Qatar, Land of Blessing'

But in fear of feeling uneasy, bearing it,
At last like foolish men,
We bursted into a laugh with Ha, Ha, Ha. from closed mouth.

- Tr. by Won Eung-soon

Note: 1) cuttle fish mixed with vinegar
2) special restaurant for reservation
3) tasty green onion grilled

베트남 하노이에서

이슬비 내리는 하노이 거리에
장대비 퍼붓듯 쏟아지는 오토바이 행렬
숨 막힌 위험 속 아슬아슬 곡예사님들
여기서 툭 저기서 툭 불쑥불쑥 오토바이
조인 가슴 놀라고 화도 나련마는
그 건 당연한 듯 투정도 없이
기다리고 비켜가는 너그러운 님 들
여유 있는 그 모습에 감동 박수 보냅니다.

한참을 다니다가 허기진 배 채우려
물어물어 찾은 정겨운 한국식당
베트남 사장님의 서툰 한글 메뉴판에
미소 머금은 내 눈길 머물러 돌고
입술만 벙긋벙긋
'오징어부무침(오징어초무침), 예약몽문(예약전문),
맛있는 파산(맛있는 파전)'
이걸 어쩜 좋아 웃음이 곧 터질 것 같은데
그들이 알면 무안해 할 수도 있는데
결국 바보처럼
다문 입 웃음보따리 푸 푸 풋 터지고 말았습니다.

The Black Butterfly Dances on the Rose

A black butterfly
On the black rose flower
Dances waveringly
In the midsummer's burning heat.

The black butterfly as if it's seen or not,
Stretching its wings on the rose blossoms
Dancing its slender waist,
Sends the hot weather behind us
In order to cool it off.

- Tr. by Won Eung-soon

Kim Ji-yeul/Korea

* Graduated from The College of Chemistry in Joseon University.
* Finished The Graduate School of Jeonnam University(master of science) and that of Catholic Medical College(doctor of medicine).
* A professor of Jeonnam Medical College.
* The president of The Korean Nuclear Medicine Academy(1996~ 1998)
* Address : 160, Ilsim-ri, Hwasun-eup, Hwasun-gun, Jeon-nam, 519-809, Korea

검정 나비 장미꽃 위에 춤추고

하늘을 불태우는 삼복 더위에
검정 나비 하나
검은 장미꽃 위에
하늘거리며 춤을 춘다

보일 듯 말 듯한 검정 나비
가는 허리 춤추는 장미
꽃송이 위에 나래를 펴고
한 더위를 식혀 주려
이 더위를 뒤로 보낸다.

A Stone Within Me

There is a stone shining secretly within me
Who am dark and deep.

It
Only opens my way,
Leads me to myself
Lest I should move to some other things
Except me.

Also it
Makes me run well
Not to fall down,
And makes my way upright
And makes my eyes bright.

Kim Jong-hee/ Korea

* Born in Cheonju City, Chungbuk, Korea.
* Graduated from Dept. of English Lit. of Yonsei University.
* First Debut as a Poet through "the Poetics" monthly magazine(1982).
* A Member of Writer's Association of Korea, International Pen Club, and the Good Literature Club.
* A Committee for Guidance of Modern Poet's Association.
* Director of Member's Club of Poetics.
* Prize from "the Poetics" monthly magazine.
* Address: 337-36 Seokyodong, Mapogu, Seoul, Korea
* Phone: 02-335-0264(Home), 011-229-0264(Handphone)

But it is the stone disclosing
Only when I alone enter the deep cave of the soul,
And look into it silently,
And that is a gem untouched by time,
It's only one star within me in the world.

- Tr. by Won Eung-soon

내 안의 돌

어둡고 깊은 내 안에
숨어서 반짝이는 돌이 하나 있지

그것은
내가 나 이외의 어떤 다른 것에
가 닿지 않게
오직 내 길을 열고
나를 내게로 인도하지

또한 그것은
내가 넘어지지 않게
내가 잘 달릴 수 있게
내 길을 곧게 하고
내 눈을 밝게 하지

그러나 그것은 홀로
영혼의 깊은 동굴 속으로 들어가
가만히 들여다보아야만 보이는 돌
시간이 손대지 못하는 보석
세상에서 단 하나뿐인 내 안의 별이지

A Flight of Dream

In lonesome day
Binding on the stake of actuality,
I become a salmon returning to his home stream.

In the sunshine of late spring, hung down on the shaggy dog's back,
The tree-made body of a mortar dozing at a corner of the storehouse,
And the piling firewood in line at the corner of the yard,
I already become a boy hanging around the yard.

The jar's water drops of my sweet drenching her head,
The rumination of 'a yellow cow' closed eyes at the stable,
And the black pig snorting faster than quicken my pace,
Make a colorful picture.

Kim Kye-shik/ Korea

* Pen Name: Youngjoo
* Member of the Korean Writers' Association
* Director of Poets' Association of Jeonbuk, Korea
* Member of Institute of Future Culture in Korea
* Editor of Han-All Literature
* Adviser of Jeonbuk Branch, International Pen Club
* Member of the World Poetry Institute
* Conferred the Order of National Service Merit and received a great prize of 'Chang-jo' Literature, and the President Prize of G.C.S. International Club, and the Main Prize of Jeonbuk PEN Literature
* Served as a Principal of Maryung High School, as a Director of Jeonbuk Educational Institute
* Published such Poetical Anthologies titled as 'Love as River', 'Steal a Glance at the World' 'An Annual Ring', 'Stepping Stones', 'Bamboo Trees Grows Together and 'The Soliloquy of a Snail' etc.
* Address: 102-901 Kolong "Haneulchae Apt", No.55# Wanshan-Gu, Jeonju-si, Jeon-buk
* Tel: 063-901-2727(House), 010-9774-2727(H.P) * E-Mail: kskim39@hanmail.net

When I looked a far-off mountain sitting at a corner of the town,
Dashing sound of the running rats,
The sound of fulling cloth,
And grinding grain in a stone mill between mother-in-law and daughter-in-law,
Make all longings surging in my deep heart.

Though the mother salmon already
Closes her eyes lingeringly
Because of her youngs thrown themselves in her arms,
She becomes a bird flying lightly over the sky.

- Tr. by Won Eung-soon

꿈의 비상(飛翔)

울적한 날에는
현실의 말뚝에 몸 매어 두고
모천에 회귀하는 연어가 된다

삽살개의 등 위에 늘어진 늦봄 햇살
허청 구석에서 졸고 있는 나무 절구통
토방 모서리에 가지런히 쌓인 장작더미
나는 벌써 마당 서성이는 소년이 되고

영의 귀밑머리 적시던 물동이의 물방울
외양간 눈감은 누렁이의 되새김질
발걸음보다 더 빨리 꿀꿀대던 꺼먹돼지
채색 짙은 한 폭의 그림이 된다

도시 모서리에 걸터앉아 먼산바라기 할 때
중천장 줄다름치던 쥐들의 뜀박질소리
귀 안에 아련히 들려오는 다듬이소리
고부간 어처구니 맞잡아 빗어대는 맷돌소리
저 마음 깊숙한 곳 잔잔히 밀려오는 그리움

어미 연어는
가슴팍 파고드는 새끼들로
시름시름 눈 감겨도
몸 가벼이 하늘 나는 한 마리 새가 된다.

The Full Story of Flowers

In order to bloom a flake of the flower,
They has to pass wind, to be exposed to the weather,
To face with the hot sunshine,
When the harsh wind blows,
They get rent and broken in end,
And all its leaves and blossoms fall down shedding tears.

The flowers in a greenhouse blooms easy and comfortably,
But other ones out of it like weeds
Get trampled down and are stamped out,
None the less, the flowers bloom beautifully without fail,
Who(no body) knows their inner mind?

But
The past years that tormented them so hard ,
Are all needful trials in blooming,
And only the flowers putting up with them,
Bloom colorfully in all seasons, bearing fruits in autumn,
So they prepare a happy feast for the fruits nest year,
This is the full story of flowers.

- Tr. by Won Eung-soon

Kim Kye-yoon/Korea

* Graduated from The College of Medicine in Jeonnam University.
* Finished The Graduate School of Jeonnam University(M.D.).
* The president of the southern branch of The International Wise Man.
* Awarded the golden prize of Red Cross Philanthropy Prize.
* Debut through "Jigu Munhak" by essays.
* A member of The World Poetry Research Institute.
* Published a poetical works entitled "A Dreamy Hwangryong River"
* Address : Kim Hospital, 161-2, Daemin-dong, Dong-gu, Gwangju-si, Korea

꽃들의 사연

한 송이 꽃을 피우기 위해
바람도 스쳐가고 눈비도 맞아 보고
따가운 햇살도 받아 보고
모진 칼바람 휘두르면
결국 찢기고 부러지고
그러다가 잎도 꽃도
다~ 떨어져 서러운 눈물도 마셔 본다

온실 안의 어느 꽃은 호강 받으며 피우는데
온실 밖 또 한 꽃은 천덕꾸러기 잡초처럼
짓밟히고 뽑혀나가고
그래도 기어코 화사하게 피워내는
아름다운 꽃들의 시린 속내 뉘 알리오

그러나
그리도 괴롭혔던 지나간 세월은
꽃 피는데 다~ 필요했던 시련들
고통에서 잘 버티어준 그 꽃들이
철따라 울긋불긋 예쁘게도 피어서
이듬해 피울 씨앗까지 영글어두고
행복한 열매 잔치 꽃들의 사연

Dokdo Isle on the Dining Table

At the time of evening, darkness is falling
At the round table we sat around like a folding screen
Spreads an acrid or slightly bitter fragrance of wild edible greens spreads
And our hands with chopsticks move as busy as the conductor of orchestra.

We don't feel envy of the royal meal with all sorts of tasty delicacies,
A mackerel in the sea folds its wings,
Some pieces of bean-curds as decorative seasonings take after Dokdo Isle.
That remains as a piece of landscape in the boundless sea upon a dish.

In it
Birds, clouds, and winds stand,
And a guard stepping on the waving sea
Clears the table quickly smiling on a contented lip.

- Tr. by Won Eung-soon

Kim Kyeong-soon/Korea

* Poet
* Graduated from Graduate School of Culture and Inheritance, Gongju Univ.
* Member of Korea Headquarters, International Pen Club
Member of Korean Writers' Association
* Vice president at the Newspaper of Literature
* Director of the World Poetry Institute
* Received a prize of the Literary Art and Trend and a great Prize of Reading Books
* Poetical Anthology: "The Rhapsody of a Night"

밥상 위의 독도

어둠이 깔리는 저녁 어귀
병풍처럼 둘러앉은 두레상에
아린 듯 쌉싸름한 산채향기 피어나고
젓가락 오케스트라 지휘하듯 분주하다

입맛 이끄는 산해진미 수라상이 부럽잖고
바다 속을 누비던 고등어도 날개 접고 나란히
고명 얹은 두부토막 독도를 닮아 있다
접시 위 망망대해에 홀로 남은 풍경 한 점

그 속에서
새와 구름 바람들이 일어선다
파도치는 난바다에 발 딛고 선 파수장이
포만한 모습 입가에 미소 일 때 밥상을 얼른 치운다

A Whetstone

There is a being who peeks off the fault of the mossy vicious mind,
Lifting up the buried time lightly,
Sacrificing itself unsparingly.

Because of incurable pains like a bruise,
Even if flowing out black or red tears sluggishly,
There is a life training
Stronger than its own body devoting its body.

Though wearing out its own body at odd moments,
For the bright instant,
For the brighter instant,
It's the destiny to live confronting many things.

Perhaps
Even if its life staking and devoting its all existence,
Is being corroded,
There is a loftiness weeping for its dearest wish,
For somebody to kiss at painful wound,
For the other rebirth.

- Tr. by Won Eung-soon

Kim Kyung-soon / Korea

*Chairman of Hanwool Writers' Association of Korea
*Member of Korea Writers' Association
*Member of International Pen club, Korea Headquarter
*Standing Vice Director of Exchange Promotion between International Culture and Art
*Won a great Prize of Literature(Poetry), as a Contributor for Korea Literature , 2011
*Publication: "Wishing to Go to You as Wind" / "The Moon Fallen into the Lake"

숫돌

이끼 낀 사념(邪念)의 허물 벗겨 내고
푹 꺼진 시간 번쩍번쩍 들어 올리며
아낌없이 자신을 내어 주는 존재가 있다

치유할 수 없는 피멍 같은 통증으로
검은 혹은 붉은 눈물 질펀히 흘러도
제 몸 바쳐
제 몸보다 더
강한 힘으로 연마(硏磨)하는 삶이 있다

시나브로 마모되어 가는 육신에도
빛나는 순간을 위하여
더욱 빛나는 순간을 위하여
무수히 부대끼며 살아가야 하는 운명

설혹
존재의 전부를 걸고 바치던 생애(生涯)
부식(腐蝕) 되어 간다 해도
누군가 또 다른 부활을 위하여
아픈 상처와 입맞춤하며
염원의 눈물 흘리는 숭고(崇高)가 있다.

Do You Know the Flower's Secret?

A fire broke out in the mountain of Spring
We as pierrot,
Who live changing our faces every year,
Didn't burn ourselves for want of fire's source,
We had better burn even to the roots.
To be in full bloom and to wither
Are only a process of pains.
Burn vigorously, burn out.
To laugh looking at us,
Who exist to be trodden on with feet,
Burn out vigorously, vigorously,
Ah it will be too, too clear and quick.
Such a flower's life as has to endure pains as a fixture
Was very merciless, and very harsh.

- Tr. by Won Eung-soon

Kim Kyung-hee / Korea

*The 3rd Daughter of the Resistance Poet Kim Ak in Gwang-Ju City.
*A Member of the Literary Men's Association of Korea; of the Modern Poets Association.
*Vice Chairman of the Literary Movement & Trend; A Editor of Gangseo Literary Association of Seoul.
* Chief Editor of Eulji Publishing Corporation
*Received the Prize of Literature of the Literary Movement & Trend.
*Anthology: <The Beautiful Scolding>, <The Soul Sketch in Soul>, etc..
*Address: 1269, Guro-Bondong, Gurogu, Jungang Apt., 10-1901, Seoul.

꽃의 속내를 아시는가?

봄 산에 불이 붙었다
해마다 얼굴 바꾸며 사는
삐에로 우리들
불씨 없어 불타지 못했는데
뿌리까지 태워지면 좋겠다
만개도 시듦도
고초의 과정일 뿐이다
타라~ 훨훨 타오르거라
즈려 밟혀 사는
아픈 우릴 보고 웃더니
타라 훨훨 훨훨~
아아 너무너무 시원하겠다
풍파 감내하는 붙박이 꽃살이
참으로 가혹하고 가혹하였다

One Hundred Years' Longing

With the sound of bamboo's wind for one hundred year,
Into the deep darkness
Through a long tunnel
A longing sprouts.

To be attracted for you,
Being carved in your joints
Is a sway
Filled with secrets.

The painful tremor of blueness
Crosses over the sea with the wind,
The camellia of one hundred year,
Having got over the fierce storm and coldness,
Is stuck in your heart.

Kim Mi-kyoung/Korea

* Born at Gangjin, Jeon-Nam, Korea.
* Graduated from Dept. of the National Language and Literature of the Air and Correspondence College of Korea.
* An Authorized Intermediary(Present).
* Recommended As a Poet from the Monthly 'the Literary Movement & Trend'.
* A Member of the World Poetry Research Institute

On the day
When one hundred year's longing soaked in,
The red camellia bloomed,
The grand force of your attraction
Wiggled even the universe.

- Tr. by Won Eung-soon

백년 그리움

백년 대바람 소리
깊은 어둠 속
긴-터널에서
그리움은 싹트고

마디마디 다져진
그대 향한 끌림은
공명(空冥) 가득한
하늘거림이어라

시린 푸르름의 진동은
바람에 실려 바다 건너고
폭풍과 혹독한 추위 지난
백년 동백
그대 심장에 박힌다

백년 그리움 스며든 날
붉은 동백 피어나고
끌림의 거대한 힘은
우주가 그만,
꿈틀거렸어라

A Yoke

Always from my bosom
The white blood runs down.
In a rainy day or a snowy day
It's milky white blood spouting as white as the pear blossoms,
Scattering in the rainy wind from its bosom.

Father's tears for his children
Worrying about in a foreign land, from my childhood,
Was changed into sand like a rock to be white blood of my bosom,
And soaked into heart, and into heart again
To be a sad song of my father in the sandy wind.

My father was my icon,
Every night of the bright moon, I imagined father's smile in my mind,
And in night of the shining stars, father's hope.
I still become a moon rotating along his orbit.

Kim Min-jung/Korea

* Born on Feb. 17, 1951. Sanwemyon, Jeongeup city
* Started a literary career through 'Literary Movement & Thought'
* A secretary general of jeonbuk branch of Korean free poetry literary men's association
* A director of the organization of Literary Movement & Thought
* A vice-president of jeonbuk branch of 'Literary Movement & Thought'
* Address : 442-2, Pyeongsa-ri, Sanoe-myeon, Jeongeup-si, Jeonbuk, 580-950, Korea

I wish to live, now desiring as a father to my children
In order to bloom beautiful and charming flowers
And to bear fruits, on a winy day
To be a branch of a weeping willow.

- Tr. by Won Eung-soon

멍에

나의 가슴에는 항상 하얀 피가 흐른다
비 오는 날이나 눈 오는 날엔
비바람에 흩어지는 배꽃처럼
온 가슴에서 멍울멍울 뿜어 나는
우윳빛 하얀 피

유년 시절 타향에서 바라보던
자식을 향한 아버지의 눈물은
내 가슴의 하얀 피가 되어 바위를 모래화하고
모래 바람 속의 황량한 아버지의 노래 되어
다시 가슴으로 가슴으로 스며들었다

아버지는 나의 우상이었다
달이 밝은 밤에는 아버지의 웃음을
별이 빛나는 밤이면 아버지의 희망을 그렸다
난 아직도 궤적을 따라 자전하는 달이 된다

이제 내가 아비 되어 아이들에게는
곱고 탐스러운 열매 꽃으로 피어나도록
바람 부는 날 수양버들가지 되어
염원하고 또 염원하며 살고 있지만

The Falling Camellia Blossom

Flowers
Are filthy out of season,
Only bright in season.

You lying red
At the behind wall of Sunwoon Temple,
Are more heartrending in autumn ground.

The weight of fruiting yearning
Is fruited grain by grain and piled up
With winds of a pine in May or June,

The full story beyond words
Listening to it,
Inwardly, inwardly,
Became a sound of copper bell

Kim Sang-kyung/ Korea

* Pen name: Hyang Myung
* Born at Asan, Kochang, Jeonbuk, Korea
* Studied under the Poet, Shin Seok-jeong
* Made a Debut as a Poet from 'the Literary Arts and Trend'
* Vice Chairman of Yangcheon Literary Association
* A Defence Committee of Copyrights in Korean Writers' Association, and of a Member of the Modern Poets' Association.
* A Commander of Shinwol No. 2 District at Uangcheon Police Station
* Won a great Prize for an Impromptu Poem at a Literary Writing Contest
* Address: 361-1 Hwagok 1-dong, Kangseo-gu, Hwagok Daelim Apt. 5-1504, Seoul
Tel: 010-6211-2100(H.P.)

The red sister of Sunwoon Temple!

You, lying in heart broken,
Are now redder than twilight,
The lonesome heart has been bruised.

- Tr. by Won Eung-soon

동백 낙화

꽃은
때 넘으면 누추하고
때에 찬란하다

선운사 뒷 담장
붉어 누운 그대는
갈 땅에서 더 눈물겹네

맺혀 버린 그리움의 무게
알알이 뭉치고 포개지어
오뉴월 솔바람 소리

귀 기울이다
말 못할 사연은
속으로 속으로
동종소리 되었구려

선운사 붉은 누이여!

가슴 저며 누운 지금
낙조보다 붉으니
외진 가슴
멍이 들어 버렸다오

The Confused World

Whose words are right?
It's a missile without the right answer.
It secedes from the track in a roaring sound.
The world is swarming,
Brethren has no way because of its homogeneity,
There are many people to repeat a great absurd show.

It's the confused world,
After being awake, suicide, detention,
The public officials extort general trader's money, or evade their tax,
Truly, is it a world to make an attempt to live?

Kim Seok-ki/Korea

* Pen Name: Il-Mook.
* Graduated from the Air and Correspondence College.
* Recommended As a Poet from the Literary Magazine of 'the Han-Wul Literature'.
* A Member of the Literary Men's Association of Korea; of the International Pen Club in Korea.
* A Member of the World Poetry Research Institute of Korea.
* An Official at the Health Insurance Corporation(Present).
* Poetical Anthology: "Thou Sunk in My Soul"/ "Sailing With a Fare Wind"
* Won the Prize of the Monthly "the Han-Wul Literature"/ and a great Prize of "the Keum Ho Literature"/ and the Crown Prize for 100th Anniversary of the Hyundaimunhak, Monthly Magazine/ and a great Prize for the Completed Poet from the Newspaper of the Korean Literature
* Co-publisher of the Quarterly magazine "the Renaissance Movement", The Promotion Fund for the Korean Literature (present)
* E-mail: sksanai@hanmail.net/ 010-4062-3652
* daum blog: http://blog.daum.net/sksanai
* Address: (425-838)Singil-jungangro 4-gil 6-303, Danwongu, Ansan City, Gyeonggi-do, Korea

It's the world it's no use to remorse our life,
Face to face confrontation, and internal troubles.
A servant is only as honest as his master,
But the upstream pollutes downstream by its night soil.

We should stick to the historical view on our nation
As the high monk keep the exorcist's dance.
So we should not dance the free or rough dance,
Beating time with other powerful country, not our proper one.
Without any tender and warm emotion of ours,
We stand all in front of dreadful winds with no spirits.

- Tr. by Won Eung-soon

혼란스런 세상

누구 말 올바른 말인가
정답 없는 미사일
굉음 속 궤도 이탈한다
세계는 들끓고,
동포란 동질성 때문에 속수무책
엄청난 쇼를 서슴없이 반복하는 사람들

혼란스런 세상
자고나면 자살, 억류
누구 돈, 세금 등쳐먹고,
과연 살아 볼만한 세상인가
후회막급인 인생살이
극과 극의 대결, 그리고 내분
물은 위에서 아래로 흐르는데
윗물이 탁류로 개울을 적신다

고승이 살풀이춤을 고수하듯
조국의 역사성을 찾아야 한다
강대국 장단에 맞춰 우리 고유의 춤 아닌
막춤을 추어선 되겠는가
우리네 정답고 따뜻한 정서는 간곳없고
칼바람 앞에 혼을 놓고 서 있다.

In A Dessert 6

There is a way also in the heaven.
As far as we know the countless stars in the universe
Turn around their own orbit ceaselessly without colliding with one another,
The stars know their own way definitely too.

As far as we know the stars turn around
That grand space of the universe orderly
Without an inch of error,
They also seem to know the natural law.

In this world
For us to be entangled, baffled, and in discord,
Is due to our ignorance about our ways.

Why do we live with not knowing the way,
That the stars know already?
The stars were crying,
And my eyes filled with tears.

- Tr. by Won Eung-soon

Kim So-youb/Korea

* Recommended As a Poet from the Literary Magazine 'the Han Kook Literature'.
* A Member of the Modern Poets Association; of the International Pen Club; of the Literary Men's Association of Korea
* Director of the Woman's Literary Society of Korea.
* Chair Professor of Department of Creative Writing, Daejun University
* President of the Whole Christian Culture Art Association of Korea(Present)
* Poetical Anthology: <Thou Rising As a Star>with others.
* Collection of Essays: <The Green Color Life>with others.
* Address: 261, Chungsoodong ,Chunan City, Chung-Nam, Sunkyung Apt. 112-601.
* E-mail: kimsoyeop@yahoo.co.kr * Mobile: 010-2440-6615

사막에서 6

하늘에도 길이 있다
우주의 무수한 별들이 부딪히지 않고
자기의 궤도를 부단히 돌고 있는 걸 보면
별들도 자기 길을 분명 알고 있다

저 광대한 우주 공간을
한 치 오차도 없이
질서정연하게 돌고 있는 걸 보면
별들도 우주의 이치를 알고 있는 것 같다

우리가 세상에서
엉키고 빗나가다 부딪히는 것은
자기네 길을 제대로 몰라서일 것이다

별들도 아는 길을
왜 우리는 모르며 살고 있는 것일까
별이 울고 있었다
내 눈도 눈물이 고였다

The Outdoor Lamp

You are awaiting the exhausted souls.
When it rains by chance,
All the wet hearts are flowing
Like a river in darkness.

You, returning in exhausion,
After erasing the day's disguise,
Can you not hear the rhythm of Brahms,
Sounding all night long?

If you term the yearning
As sorrow,
I merely give a send-off

Kim Song-bae / Korea

* start a literary career after winning a prize for a new writer held by 'Simsang'
* a member of the Korea Writer Association(poetry dept)
* an executive director of The World Writer's Member Club
* a director of international pen club Korean headquarters
* a member of the central executive committee of Mokwol Literature
* a principal of Cheongsong Poetry Creation Academy
* received prizes (Tami literature, Peace Literature,
* published books (poetical works entitled A Volume of a Space Poem and 9 others, critical essay entitled Study of Space Poetry and 4 others, A Method of Creating a poem and 2 others, a collection of essays entitled 'Is It a Intellect or Sincerity Moving the Skies to Tears' and 4 others.

* Address: 112-44, naresilgil 40-1, yeonhee 1-dong, seodaemun-gu, Seou,l Korea
* Pone No: 02-336-8188, 010-3797-8188

To the exhausted souls,
Being unable to give them
A tender word,
Standing alone in my dim garden.

- Trans. by Joon-young Lee

외등(外燈)

지친 영혼을 기다린다
행여 비라도 내리면
젖은 마음들이
어둠 속에 강물로 흐르고

하루의 분장을 지우면서
부서져 돌아가는 사람아
밤새도록 흔들리는
브라암스의 선율이 들리는가

그리운 것들이 슬픔이라면
희미한 내 뜨락에서
따사로운 언어 하나
안겨주지 못한 채
지친 영혼들을 그냥 떠나 보낸다.

In a hill at the back

A fragrant air,
it urges my hurried steps.
Waves of light green like a cotton candy among a straight pine trees,
it looks like a warm heart of the lord.

White cheery flowers give me a joy.
So soon, light pink petals of a tall royal azalea,
they step up to me as flapping the wings of angel

Cuckoo cuckoo
Ppie ppie ppie ppieee~~
Huyo huyoo huyihu
Ziri ziri zoruririk
Kuy kuy
Wa a a aa
Sacred choir in a forest

Kim Sun/Korea

* Born in Seoul
* Studied at Songshin Women's University,
Graduate School of Songshin Women's University,
Graduate School of Seoul National University, majored Piano.
* Studied at Korea National Open University, majored English language literature
* Debuted through Gigu Literature Journal
* Address: 301 Ho, 105 Dong, Joyparkvill, 139-6, NamSan-ri, PaengSeong-eub, PyeongTaek-Si, Gyeonggi-do, 451-803, Korea.

It is spread through a forest
with sliding a tiny rill like spring water
Give me the full holy spirits,
be taken me in the thing
that makes the lord happy,
and give me a domestic heaven
that continually praise and service.
Thanking you for today's all the things.

뒷산에서

향긋한 내음
바쁜 걸음 재촉하고
곧은 소나무 사이로
솜사탕 같은 연둣빛 물결
따스한 주님의 마음 같다

하이얀 벚꽃이
기쁜 마음 던져 주고
어느새 키 큰 철쭉의 연분홍 꽃잎들이
천사의 날갯짓으로 다가온다

뻐꾹뻐꾹
삐이삐이 삐이~~~
휘이 후오 휘이후
찌리찌리쪼르리릭
꺼~이 꺼~이
워어어 어어
숲속 성가대

생수 같은 산 개울 따라
숲속에 싸여 울려 퍼진다
오늘 이 모든 것 감사하며
성령 충만하게 해 달라고
주님 기쁘시게 하는 일에
쓰임 받게 해 달라고
찬양과 예배가 끊이지 않는
가정 천국 이루게 해달라고

At A Well-Side

At a well-side before the yard,
I draw water with a bucket,
And dip up a love.

Beyond the well-side
An orchid is modest and gentle with lowered head,
And mother smiles quietly.

Mother, stepping on dewdrops
And going round to see me ordinary,
I feel something lacking of her
As if I count stars in the sky.

Before he violet orchid
Drops its petals,
Mother, come again,
Making a friend with moon.

- Tr. by Won Eung-soon

Kim Whoa-ja / Korea

* Poet. Born in Chungbuk, Korea.
* Graduated from National Lang& Lit. of Busan University.
* A Member of KBS Chorus.
* Director of Korea Woman's System.
* First Debut as a Poet through "Literary Movement & Trend"
* A Member of the World Poetry Research Institute, Baekma Literature, Daejeon Poets' Association(Present).
* Received the Literature Prize of the World Poetry Institute

* Address: 487, Sajeong-dong, Joong-gu, Woonamstawon 101-801, Daejeon City.

우물가에서

뜨락 앞 우물에서
두레박으로 물을 긷는다
사랑을 퍼 올린다

우물가 저만치에서
난초가 다소곳하다
어머니가 조용히 웃는다

이슬을 밟고
일상처럼 다녀가시는 어머니
별을 세는 것처럼
아쉬움을 남기신다

보랏빛 난(蘭)이
꽃잎을 떨구기 전에
달을 친구 삼아
어머니, 다시 찾아오세요

At the Weekend Farm

As if the grasses and vegetables
Are mixed up to grow thickly at the vegetable field,
My mind,
Was so mixed up with truth, lies, hypocrisy, and falsehood
To grow thickly.

After weeding a field all the day,
As if the vegetables only then expose their real looks,
The lies, hypocrisy, and falsehood through weeding them
Was so exposed as truthful mind.

When I saw them lining up in one file, smiling one another,
My mind was full.
Yes, that's right.
As if we weeded the vegetables field,
I should pull up weeds of my mind.

- Tr. by Won Eung-soon

Kim Young-mi / Korea

* Pen name: Da-In
* A poet, an essayist
* A member of the Korea Writers' Association
* A member of Pen Club in Korea Headquarters
* A director of the magazine "Literature & consciousness
* A chief editor of a quarterly magazine "Modern selected poems
* The chief director of the Image Literature in Korea
* Awarded] Heonan Heosol prize in 2006
* Awarded a distinguished service medal from the magazine "Literature & consciousness
* A thesis : A Strategy for self protection and existence, and so on

* Address: #417-3 Seok-Su 2dong, Manan-Gu, Anyang City, Dusan-We've, @110-103, Gyeonggi-do, Korea.

주말 농장에서

마치 남새밭에
풀과 남새가 뒤범벅되어 무성하듯이
내 마음은
진실과 거짓과 위선과 허위가
뒤범벅되어 무성하게 자라고 있었다.

하루 종일 풀을 매고 나니
그제서야 남새가 제 모습을 드러냈듯이,
내 마음속의 거짓과 위선과 허위를
김매기 해야 진실한 마음이 드러나겠지.

가지런히 줄맞추어 선 남새를 보니
빙그레 미소를 짓는 듯하여 뿌듯하다.
그래
남새밭을 가꾸듯이
내 마음도 자주자주 잡풀을 매어야겠다.

A Rebellion of Three Feet

Toward his fierce struggle for existence
We sprinkle a few cups sea-water as a comfort.
Every tentacle, hacked to pieces, adhering his sucker to the thing,
As it is a guillotine, without knowing it,
Gives a shriek wiggling.
From the other side of the world,
His ways, walking on three feet
In order to get the big desire,
So are forced to abandon himself to his fate in the mud.
To wash a octopus
Is to look into the center of the sea,
While we are feeling after the black heart of the sea's inside,
Not to disclose before us, in advance,
Wine is long to be congealed for the supper,
Prepared with only a few cold cups on the plastic dishes,
On further reflection, youth had always a forked road.

Kim Young-mi/Korea

* Pen name: Sim-Jeon
* Born at Chung-Ju, Chung-Buk, Korea.
* Recommended As a Poet from the Literary Movement & Trend.
* A Member of the Literary Men's Association of Korea.
* An Auditor of Gwangju Branch of the Whole Art Federation of Korea.
* Director of the Publication of Gwangju Literary Men's Association .
* Poetical Anthology: The Trampled Earthworm Cuts the Paralyzed Past, etc.
* Address: 422-1 Sam-Lee, Gonjiam-Eup, Hyun-yeunrip B-dong, #103, Kwangju City, Kyunggi-do, Korea

When many people wanted to go for the wider sea,
Some of them tried to find the truth into the mud,
And I tried to convey the story of the deep sea to the other side of the world.
When the truth into the mud shakes,
I bring in my dry heart,
Carrying the long and fine stories in the salted wind of the sea.
Some where in the world, the sharp language of mine
May be a guillotine for myself.
So I try to stick my sucker of my poetry to the plastic world.
To wash a octopus
Is a solace of youth walking on three feet,
And is to wash out the black heart piled up on a byway,
Returning it to the sea, the soule of poetry.

- Tr. by Won Eung-soon

세발의 반란

치열한 생존의 몸부림에
몇 톨의 바다를 위로처럼 뿌려 준다
단두댄 줄도 모르고 빨판을 밀착시키던
난도당한 촉수마다 흡착된 비명이 꿈틀댄다
세상 저쪽에서
커다란 욕망을 실으려 했던
세발로 걸어온 길들은
저토록 뻘 속에서 제 운명을 내 놓는가
낙지를 씻는 일은
바다의 중심을 들여다보는 일
쉽사리 내주지 않던 바다 속 흑심을 짐짓 더듬는 사이
술은 응고된 지 오래
프라스틱접시가 싸늘한 잔 몇 개를 장만하는 저녁,
돌이켜보면 청춘은 늘 갈림길이었지
많은 이들이 더 넓은 바다로 향할 때
몇몇은 진흙 속 진리를 찾으려 했고
난 심해의 사연을 세상 저쪽까지 전하려 했다
뻘 속 진리가 흔들릴 때면
마른 가슴에 바다를 불러들이며
염분 섞인 바람에 밋밋한 사연을 실어 보낸다
세상 어딘가에선 날선 내 언어가
스스로의 단두대가 될지도 모를 일
시혼의 빨판을 플라스틱 같은 세상에 밀착시켜 본다
낙지를 씻는 일은
세발로 걸어온 청춘의 위로며
뒷길에 쌓아둔 흑심을 헹궈
시혼의 바다로 되돌려 보내는 일이다

My Mistress

Today the piercing pain on you
Is ripening surely as a longing.

Really,
Is the love painful so?
The love is left even in the barefooted crude life,
For all my efforts, cutting it off or erasing to forget it,

Your image was passing by as swift as a fire,
But I knew that the fire is not died out,
However making efforts, to die it out.

Even in spite of violent wind and rain, it shows its own real character
So, in the picture of Leonardo da Vinci,
I can see the painful love.

Being caught by its waves,
Should I go together with delights and pains like destiny(karma)
As if the wind does so, in hiding itself.

- Tr. by Won Eung-soon

Ko Bang-kyu / Korea

* Born at Okjeri, Sungnaemyun, Gochang, Jeon-Buk.
* Graduated from Dept of Literary Art of Masan Changshin University.
* Retired from the Managing Materials of Changwon Factory in Han Hwa Group.
* Recommended As a Sijo Poet from the Sijo Literature, 2003.
* A Member of the Lierary men's Association of Korea; of the World Poetry Research Institute of Korea; the Literary Coterie ' Soorim'; of A Consultant of the New Age Literature.
* Poetical Anthology: <A Love As Rose Flower>.

* Address: 463, Okjeri, Gochanggun, Jeon-Buk, Korea.

그대

오늘도 그대의 사무친 아픔은
또록 또록 그리움으로 영글어갑니다

진정
사랑은 이렇게 아픈 건가
맨발로 거친 삶을 살아도 사랑은 지워지지 않는다는 것을
뭔가 그토록 잊으려 애써 깎고 찍어 지워 버리려도

불꽃처럼 스쳐가는 그대의 모습이었습니다
인제는 불꽃을 끄고 싶어도
꺼지지 않은 것이 사랑이란 것을 알았습니다

비 바람 몰아쳐도 사랑은 속살을 드러냄이다
다빈치의 그림 속에서도 사랑의
아픈 상처가 보입니다

물결처럼 휘감아
아픔도 기쁨도 함께 숙명처럼 안고 가야 하나요
제 몸을 드러내지 않는 바람결처럼 -

An Age of Loss

The city that darkness faded away and the silence was broken,
A limpid light was not died out,
Lots of unsleeping lives
Refuse to bear fruits, stopping to love.

In night, the old tacit promise
Summoning families together under a little light,
Has been broken.

It's the rebellion of light, engulfed the night,
In a boisterous dance of daylight in nights with the midnight sun
The star, moon, dream, and retrospects hided themselves.

Under the psychically gorgeous lighting.
Menacing the night of humankind,
The foolish tiger moths
Are piled high up in the cold smile.

- Tr. by Won Eung-soon

Kou Sun-ja / Korea

* Committee of Public Information in the Association of Creative Literature and Reciting Poems of Korea
* Director of the Literary Society of Nature
* Guro Writer's Association of Korea
* Member of the Writers' Association of the Literary Trend & Movement
* Member of the World Poetry Institute
* Address: 1st floor, 14-194 Gonghandong, Kangseogu, Seoul, Korea
* Mobile Phone: 010-4742-8545* E-mail: ksjmomo@hanmail.net

상실시대

어둠 사라지고 정적도 깨진 도시,
초롱한 불빛 꺼지지 않아
잠들지 못한 생명들
사랑을 멈추고 열매 맺기를 거부한다

저녁이면 작은 불빛 아래로
가족을 불러 모으던
오랜 무언의 약속은 허물어 졌다

밤을 삼켜 버린 빛의 반란
백야의 대낮 같은 불빛 나무에
몸을 숨긴 별, 달, 꿈 그리고 추억들

인류의 밤을 위협하는
화려한 싸이키 조명 아래
빛을 좇는 어리석은 부나비들
싸늘한 미소 수북이 쌓여간다

A Response in May

Your clothes are soaked to the skin by spring rain,
On the walking causeway beside rivulet with you,
In making eyes at each other between grass flower and a wild rose
A green shaded sorrow falls down lightly.

If friendship is deep, it's liable to fall in love.
So not expecting to get hot love between us,
As if the sleet in a severe winter is falling down,
Let's live wiping out white dusts in the dark night.

In the far desert of the raging sandy wind
I alone met a drunken elephant,
So, our leading life only picks up a scanty living.
In order to wash the outworn mountain's colors out,
Sometimes even spring rain should be poured down like hailstones.

Lee Ah-young/ Korea

* Member of the Korean Writers's Association
* Member of the Modern Poets' Association of Korea
* Director of the Open Poet's Society
* Director of the Literary Society of Nature
* Member of Writing Room of the Broadcasting for Literature
* Address: 27-3 123 Gil, Hacheon-gil, Kangbuk Province, Seoul, Korea
* H.P: 010-8253-3392
* E-mail: soochaewha@hanmail.net

This morning, I climbed up the Opae mountain near village,
The pine's colors are still more green,
And acacia-flower's fragrance, dancing like a Buddhist,
Was running far away embracing dusts in the world.

Before long a bird in a cage
Will soar up flapping its wings.

- Tr. by Won Eung-soon

5월의 화답

봄비에 옷자락 흠뻑 젖고 있네요
그대와 개울둑 산책길에서
파릇한 풀꽃과 찔래꽃 눈맞춤
녹음 짙은 슬픔 하르르 내려 앉네요

우정도 깊으면 사랑 된다잖아요
우리 뜨거운 정 서로 바라지 말고
엄동설한 진눈깨비 내리듯이
어둔 밤 하얀 먼지 씻어내며 살아요

성난 모래처럼 아득한 사막에서 나 홀로
술 취한 코끼리 만났으니
사는 일, 히치히치 할 수밖에요
오래 묵은 산빛을 거두어내려면
때론 봄비도 우박처럼 쏟아져야겠지요

오늘 아침, 동네 오패산을 오르니
솔빛 한층 더 푸르디푸르고
아카시아 꽃향기 무애(無碍)춤 추면서
홍진 껴안고 천만리 줄행랑 치네요

머지않아 새장속 새 한 마리
활개 펴고 높이 날아오를 수 있겠지요

Aroma of Yaraehyang

The emitting deep aroma
In the open mountain and field
Formerly I did not realize it far enough.

When it wakes my soul up
With its aroma
In the narrow veranda,

So had I no idea
That my dream was mature
Drunken on your emitting aroma.

O, Love, my Love,
I am sorry, so sorry
For not realize it rather earlier
That you are the aroma
Of my 'Yaraehyang'.

Lee Byung-seok / Korea

* Recommended as a poet from the Litetary Movement and Trend`
* Ph.D. of Management of Administration
* President of Samil Industry Co,Ltd.
* Consultant
* Address : 1018, Daechung Tower 13-3 Gaepo-dong. Kangnam-gu. Seoul Korea
* Moible : 010-3681-5884
* E-mail : 31ind@naber.com

O, Love, my 'Yaraehyang'!
Now you forms lucid dewdrops on the blades,
Sends a chirping of grass insects,
So I want to give the flying time
Binding in a bundle to you.

Also I am very nervous about
That the years, passing a little slow, but now
Rubbing strongly against you,
Withered your beautiful looks,
And your bright petals.

The newly emitting fragrance
Did not leave my side,
And was a constant smile,

O, Love, my Love,
Your name
Is an aroma of Yaraehyang---.

- Tr. by Won Eung-soon

야래향의 향기

드넓은 산야
짙게 피어나는 향기
예전에 미처 몰랐네

좁은 베란다에서
은밀한 향기로
내 영혼 깨울 때

모락모락 피워내는
너의 향기에 젖어
내 꿈이 영글은 것도
예전에 몰랐구나

사랑아 내 사랑아
네가 나의 야래향
향기라는 것을……
더 일찍 헤아리지 못해
미안하구나, 참 미안하구나

이제는 영롱한 이슬도 맺어 주고
풀벌레 소리도 담아 주고
날아가는 세월까지도
한 아름 묶어서 주고 싶구나
사랑아 내 야래향아

예전에 또각또각 가던 세월
그마저도 세차게 스쳐서

어여쁜 그대 모습
그 예쁘던 꽃잎을
시들게 하니 안타깝구나

새록새록 피워내는 향기는
내 곁을 지켜 주고
변함없는 미소였으니

사랑아 내 사랑아
너의 이름은
야래향 향기라는 것을……

A Sonnet on September

From a gourd's fragrance
Your figure is smeared,
And the wind on september blows at sunset
At the yard beyond the memory.

The sunlight, splitting open the door's chink
Hang down its long shadow.

The afternoon that Iris stature in the mirror
Grows much bigger,

When the quiet west wind blusters violently,
The afterimages, imbedded deeply in my bosom,
Throws its moving dance farewell,
And yet it remains its vague retrospection.

- Tr. by Won Eung-soon

Lee Chung-hee / Korea

* Made a Debut as a poet from 'the Global Literature'(2003)
* Member of the Korean Writers' Association
* Member of Guro Literary Association
* Member of "Ye-sarang" Literary Circle
* Member of Korean Race Writers' Association
* Completed the whole Course of Writing Novel
* Won the Best Prize of Literature from the Korean Race Writers' Association
* Won the Golden Prize of Heonanseolwon Literature
* Poetic Anthology: 'The White Yearning'
* Joint Poetic Works: 'A Stepstone', 'Temtation of Winds', 'Corner's Path of City', 'A Yard of Literature'
* Novel: 'Novel's Nativity', 'The Golden Feeler(Antenna)'

9월의 연가

황혼의 박꽃향기에서
너의 모습이 묻어나고
기억 저편 뜨락에 부는
9월의 바람

문틈을 비집고 들어온 햇살
그림자 길게 드리운다

거울속 아이리스의 키가
한결 커진 오후

고즈넉한 갈바람 휘감으면
가슴 깊이 박혀 있던 잔상
이별의 춤사위를 던진다 그래도
추억의 아련함은 남아 있다.

Trumpet Flower

The moaning love being entangled each other,
In covering a piece of darkness into silence,
Is seen as a mark of limpid fire.

Without pledging to meet in far future,
In a low voice as trembling,
Saying 'Good bye', sweet heart pushed my back at meandering alleys,
Now crossing an emptiness,
At every hour being put on a shadow,
Placing a piece of reddened flesh for yearning,
Why should I wait you alone all through night?

Climbing over a single pole highly,
Staying up all night of shining starlight,
The trumpet flower,
Climbing up a single pole highly,
Erasing the flowery letter of a red longing, and rewriting,
The more looking up at it with my eyes,
The more it looks as sad as a mutual love's flower
Rooting with nothing on.

- Tr. by Won Eung-soon

Lee Eun-hyup/ Korea

* Born at Cheongsan, Okcheon, Chungbuk
* Graduated from the Dept. of Atomic Energy, Hanyang Univ.
* Principal of Baekseok High School, Goyang City
* Chairman of Educational Council, Goyang Community
* Member of Korean Writers' Association * Director of Hanmaek Literary Club * General Art Union of Goyang City * Lyric Literary Writer's Association of Korea * Chairman of Literary Image Association of Korea
* (Present) Chairman of Literary Writer's Association of Goyang City
* (Present) Criminal Manipulator of Goyang District Prosecutor's Office.
* Received the Order of National Service Merit * Won a great Literary Prize of E-yuksa
* Poetic Anthology: Passing over that Mountain Tomorrow, etc.

능소화

고요 속에 어둠의 자락 덮고
서로 휘감기듯 몸 엉켜
신음하던 사랑
투명한 불의 흔적으로 보인다

먼 훗날 기약 없이
떨리는 듯 낮은 목소리로
잘 가라 등 떠밀던 굽이진 골목길
이제는 허공을 건너
그림자 하나에 얹혀오는 시간마다
그리움에 붉어진 살 한 점 놓고
어째서 저 혼자 밤 새워 기다리는가

외나무 기둥에 높이 올라
별빛 짙은 밤 지새우며
빨간 그리움의 꽃 편지
지우고 다시 쓰는 능소화
눈을 들어 바라보면 볼수록
발가벗고 서 있는 상사화처럼 애달프다.

O, Africa!
- Hope! Blooming in the Pains

The brilliant street, in red *Avishinica flowers,
The facilities of civilization are full to the brim with soaring walls of other side.
Most poor people with hungry hollow eyes
Are wriggling in the unsolved curb of poverty.

The children, roaming about the street for food to meet their empty stomach
At every time poverty and dangerous infectious disease sweep over them,
The pure souls! dying out like falling flower's petals,
Ah, there's no neighbor to shed tears for them.

It is miserable place, in which 15 years mothers with their babies
Embraced in arms are writhing in a desperate agony,
You, striving hard daily lives on their instincts

Lee Eun-mi/ Korea

* Born at Yesan, Chungcheon-bukdo, Korea
* Graduated from Korean Literature, E-wha Univ.
* Made her first Debut as a Poet from 'Munye-Sajo', Monthly Literary Magazine
* Won a Great prize for a New Poet from the Christian newspaper
* Chief Editor of 'Manmin' Quarterly Magazine
* Member of the Freedom Poet's Association of Korea
* Member of the Christian Literary Association of Korea

As it is they don't know for what, why they should exist,
And finally to end their short life!

Now because many people are shouting to search for God in heaven,
It is the place where we should plant gospels' seeds to harvest its fruits.
The providence of the loving God for salvation
Is spreading out as strong and urgent winds.

Today Africa, as our neighbor,
Usurped, plundered by thief
Is waiting for the good Samaritans.

Being wrapped and tied up their wounds
Through help of the Holy Spirit, and being prayed and wept together,
They are thirsting for the cake of flesh and the true word of soul.
(In Kenya, Africa)

- Tr. by Won Eung-soon

* Avishinica flower: It's the name of flower Africans in the field call, but the original flower's name is Nandi flame.

아프리카여!

-너 고통 속에 꽃피는 소망이여!

아비시니카 붉은 꽃망울 화려한 거리
한 쪽엔 높이 솟은 담장, 문명의 이기들 넘치건만
퀭한 눈빛 배고픈 대다수 사람들
끊을 수 없는 빈곤의 굴레 속에 몸부림치고 있다.

주린 창자 채울 곳 찾아 헤매는 어린이들
빈곤과 질병, 가혹한 전염병 휩쓸고 갈 때마다
우수수 꽃잎처럼 시들어 사라지는 순백의 영혼들이여
너를 위해 울어 줄 이웃조차 없구나.

열다섯 소녀 엄마들 홀로 아기를 안고
생존의 몸부림 처절한 곳
무엇을 위해, 왜 살아가야 하는지 알지도 못한 채
본능을 좇아 하루 생존 급급하다가
짧은 생을 마감하는 너여!

하늘 향해 부르짖으며
아버지 하나님을 찾는 이들이 유독 많은 대륙이 되었으니
희어져 추수할 곡식들이 많은 이곳
사랑의 아버지 구원의 섭리는 급하고 강한 바람처럼 펼쳐지고 있네.

오늘도 아프리카는
다 빼앗기고 상처난 강도 만난 이웃이 되어
선한 사마리아인을 기다리고 있다

성령 충만으로 상처를 싸매 주고
함께 기도하며 울어 주는
육신의 빵과 영혼의 참된 말씀을 갈급히 찾고 있다.
- 아프리카 케냐에서

* 아비시니카: 현지 시민들은 아프리카의 꽃 이름으로 부르지만 원래 꽃 이름은 난디 프레임(Nandi flame)꽃이기도 함.

Fantasy

If this world is my outing place
Such as red dragonflies are floating in the space,
Living silently with soil,

Suddenly one day
Searching that awful dream already gone far away
With the ended regret
Of my love left behind,

I would hang a hope in clear water of the Milky Way
On the edge of my life
So as to let the flower's aroma of mine fall with a thud.

- Tr. by Won Eung-soon

Lee Gang/ Korea

Lee Gang/ Korea
* Recommended as a Poet from the Monthly Magazine of the Literary Movement and Trend` 2003
* Member of the Future Literature,the Literary Movement and Trend of the Jeonbuk Writers` Association.
* Address : Saseohak-dong, Daemyeong Apt. Nadong 502, Wansan-Gu, Jeongbuk, Korea

환상

빨간 고추잠자리 허공을 떠돌 듯
이 세상이 내 놀이터라면
흙과 더불어 소리 없이 살다가

어느 날 갑자기

삭아버린 사랑의 후회만
남겨 놓은 채
아득히 떠나 가버린
그놈의 꿈을 찾아서

은하수 맑은 물에 희망을 담아
내 삶의 언저리에 걸어놓으리
내 꽃의 향기가 뚝뚝뚝

The Poet's Song

In the setting sun,
If his mind does not dye,
It's not the poet's heart.

If he looks at the moon rising in the midheaven,
But does not pick it to put in his mind,
It is not the poet's mind.

Looking at the running rain on one foot,
Or at a musical note like one autumn leaf,
Making a sound, falling down just before him,
If his heart and mind don't be opened,
He is not a poet.

The poet, not only sings a song,
But also brings up in his heart and mind
Only for chanting.

- Tr. by Won Eung-soon

Lee Ji-young/Korea

* Hyosung University of French Literature, Member of Korean Society for Literature, Member of International PEN Club in Korea Headquarters, Member of Millennium Literature Society, Vice President of the Association of Korea National Literature, Vice President of the Society of Free Poets, Received of the Korea National Literature Prize, Received of the Literary Movement & Trend Literature Prize

* Books : 'Running in grief and Want to wet like a moonlit' 'A diary on Wet day' 'A Dreaming Confidential Talk' 'The one who is easy of access and the one that discourages friendly advances' 'Holding a Mountain in one's arms" and others

* Address: Rm 1002, 311-Dong Donga Apt Dream Town, Pyeongchon-dong, Dongan-gu, Anyang-si, Gyeonggi-do, Korea

시인의 노래

낙조에
가슴이 물들지 않는다면
시인의 가슴이 아니다

중천에 뜬 달을 보고도
따 담을 줄 모르면
시인의 마음이 아니다

외발로 달려가는 빗줄기나
한 잎 보표(譜表)로 소리하며 지는
낙엽을 앞에 하고
가슴과 마음이 열리지 않는다면
시인이 아니다

시인은 노래할 뿐만 아니라
노래하기 위해
가슴과 마음에 시심을 키운다

Living As andante, andante...

While living
Let's mark with a pause
Though I lives as I keep beat with the world
Like a note running a music sheet
Without the stave

Let's live placing a rest point
On every place where mind rest

Until the end of a performance
That's enraptured at times or
Gloomy at all times
While having been living as andante, andante

Utile it perishes as a flapping bug,
Being hooked double bar at last

In the sweet time,
For my beautiful life that I love
For myself greatly
Let's spare no efforts to a pause

Lee Kyu-sae/Korea

* Started a literary career through the publication of poetical works "Autumn of that Year"
* Joint literary work: Stared again on the Road
* President of Literary Society 'P&E'
* Held Two exhibition of illustrated poems, and so on
* Address : 514-801, Jugong Apt, 702, Haan1-dong, Gwangmyeong-si, Gyeonggi-do, Korea

안단테 안단테로 살아가다가

살아가는 동안에
작은 쉼표 하나 찍고 살자
도돌이표 없는 오선지를 달리는
음표같이 세상 박자에 맞춰 살지만
마음 쉬는 곳마다 쉼표 하나 찍고 살자

수시로 황홀하고 무시로 음울한
연주가 끝나는 시간까지
안단테 안단테로 살아가다가

끝내는 겹세로줄에 걸려
파닥이는 곤충으로 숨 지는
마지막까지

그리운 시간, 죽도록 사랑하는
아름다운 내 인생을 위해
우리, 쉼표 하나 아끼지 말자.

The Sun Rising Newly

Along with the winding peaks, and the solemn sun rising above them,
I greet the new year, named Gye-sa year.
At early dawn everything begins, running along the Han riverside alone,
Also I pray to heaven, *'ip-choon-dae-gil', 'geon-yang-da-gyeong', and 'guk-tae-min-an'.
Along with the animating delight of all people and all things!

Now we run on the wide plain of Mongol
Passing over the Anryung Mountains at Daeheung,
And hearing the horse beats of the great King of 'Kwang-Gae-To' run at full speed over the continent.
With our historic hometown of our great hope to be recovered,
And with our great ancestors faced against the powers, 'Su and Dang of old Chinese Country'.

The sunlight named Chosun at the east of Asia brightens dazzlingly!
Jang Bo-go, the King of Sea, who swept the pirates,
And broke a new silk road of the sea from the Korean peninsular to the Japanese Islands,

---

Lee Sang-jin / Korea

* Born in 1941.
* Entered upon literary career through the monthly magazine "Literary Movement & Trend"
* Served the Governor of the World Poetry Research Institute.
* Serves concurrently as professor of a school of law at Dongguk University.
* Address: #306, Hangjin Building, 2478, Hwanghak-dong, Jung-gu, Seoul. 100-871, Korea

With Silla peoples established the strong trade country of the sea,
And with ancestors of southern lands having command of the sea
by the trading ships.

From the islands of south sea, Hansan, Wooldolmok, to those of
Myungryang, Noryang,
And from the sea battles of Okpo, Hansan, over that of
defeat(named a shameful battle of 7 thousand dallars), to the
Noryang sea battle,
Listen to the roaring outcries of the Chosun Battle ships with the
brave and royal soldiers of guerilla's troops,
And of the heroes of 'the Song of the Sword', who kept our sea and
saved our country.

Now in the Korean peninsular, an important position, a place of
fruit, and an axis of this globe,
We are facing the age of great change of east Asian order in the
raging waves.
The age of a complex order in 21 century is drawing near getting
out of the existing order of cold war.
We should have the wisdom to recognize our things largely and
widely with our small eyes, and lay down the high way for us all.
The second Creation has already begun to open the way of mutual
life for human-being!

- Tr. by Won Eung-soon

Note: * ip-choon-dae-gil: As one of the 24 seasonal divisions according to the lunar calender, it means Happy Blessing to all at onset of spring.
* geon-yang-da-gyeong: As one of 4 words of Chinese, it means that we pray matters calling for congratulations to all at onset of spring.
* guk-tae-min-an: It means the nation and its people enjoy the blessing of peace.

새롭게 뜨는 태양

굽이굽이 펼쳐진 연봉들 위로 떠오르는 장엄한 태양
계사년(癸巳年) 새로운 해를 맞이한다.
모든 것이 새로 시작하는 새벽, 한강변을 홀로 달리면서
입춘대길(立春大吉), 건양다경(建陽多慶), 국태민안(國泰民安)을 기원한다.
만인과 만물이 생동하는 기쁨을!

이제 우리는 대흥안령 산맥을 넘어 몽고벌판을 달린다,
대륙을 질주하던 광개토대왕의 말굽소리를 들으면서.
우리의 가슴을 뛰게 하는 회복해야 할 역사의 고향을!
중원의 수, 당 세력과 당당히 대결했던 조상님들.

아세아의 동쪽으로 내려오면 태양빛이 눈부시다!
해적들을 소탕하고
한반도와 일본열도까지 바다의 실크로드를 개척한 해상왕 장보고
무역강국, 해상상업제국을 이룩한 신라인들
무역선단을 이끌고 바다를 호령한 아랫집 조상님들

한산섬, 울돌목, 남해를 거쳐 명량, 노량까지.
옥포해전, 한산대첩을 지나, 칠천량의 치욕을 넘어 노량해전까지
불패의 게릴라부대 의병과 더불어 조선함대의 포효(咆哮)하는 함성을!
바다를 지키고 나라를 구하신 '칼의 노래'의 주인공들.

지구의 혈(穴)이며 열매 자리, 지구의 축(軸)인 한반도에선!
지금 격랑의 파고 속에 동아시아 질서의 대변환의 시기를 맞이하고 있다.

냉전질서를 벗어나 21세기 복합질서의 시대가 오고 있다.
작은 눈으로 크게 보는 지혜를! 공진(共進)의 큰길을 다져야 한다.
후천개벽이 이미 시작했음을, 상생의 길이 열렸음을!

(2012. 12. 8.)

A Horse Rider's Character

Bringing 'it' up from history,
And engraving it as a fixture
In the Kyeonbokgung subway stop,
They say it has been only 30 years.

19 months a cute baby
With blue clearly spotted bottom,
Shakes his body in a horse rider's posture
After his mama's dialect, "psy".

From a shrine of Silla's Pegasus,
Jinghis Kahn of Mongol
Seems to rush out,

Also from the "A Horse Dancing Picture"
At the wall of subway stop of Gangnam.

- Tr. by Won Eung-soon

Lee Sang-mok/Korea

*First Debut as a Poet through "The Korea Writers", & as an Essayist through "the Korea Essay".
* Served as a Lecturer at Kyung-Gi University and Myeong-Ji Univ.
* A Licensed Tax Account, Yonsei MBA.
* A Member of Korea Quarters of International Pen Club, & of Korea Writer's Association.
* Writing Books: "High Tax, Low Voice", "Living Tax". "Late Confession," etc.
* Address: 954, 2nd Floor, Dogokdong, Seoul, Korea.

기마인물상

그것을
역사 속에서 꺼내
경복궁역 승강장에
붙박이로 새겨 놓고
삼십 년이라고

볼기에 푸른 반점이 뚜렷한
열아홉 달 재롱둥이가
엄마의 "싸이"라는 말에
기마자세로 몸을 흔든다

칭기스칸이
신라 천마총에서
튀어 오를 것 같다

강남 지하역
"말 춤추는 그림"에서도

With Friends of Home Village at Sunwoon Temple

At the setting sun with a long shadow
The flowery cloud sits astraddle on the Dosol mountain,
Being proud of its beauty,

The friends, greeting in a laughing face,
We embrace them so closely as breaking heart,
And the face, met after long time silence
Wake up my memory to search for our recollection.

All delicacies of all lands and seas of home town our friends chose,
And the yellow flesh of clam being full of sea smell,
I never forgot them....

Walking along to the lane for Dosol hermitage
The flower of our stories,
Planted at the mountain's beautiful hill with wild flowers,
Was kept it in our heart,

Lim Byeong-jeon/Korea

* Born at Gochang, Jeon Buk, Korea
* Recommended as a Poet from the Gigumunhak
* Member of the Korean Writers` Association
* Member of the Poetry and Arts Association of Korea
* Director of the Writers Association of the Gigumunhak
* Secretary General of the Mapo Writers` Association
* Executive Member of O-Weol-Ae
* Poetic Anthology: The Stairs of the Paradese, etc.

After long time, when we walked together with the white frost on
our heads
And with wrinkles like earth-worms of our face,
Let’s open the skirt of our retrospection
Drinking a grog cup of wine at a tavern.

- Tr. by Won Eung-soon

선운사에서 고향 친구들과

그림자 길게 늘어진 석양에
꽃구름은 도솔산에 걸터앉아
아름다움을 뽐내고

활짝 웃는 얼굴로 반겨 주는 친구들
가슴이 터져라 안아보고
오랜만에 만난 얼굴은
추억을 뒤져가며 기억을 흔들어 깨운다

친구들이 준비한 고향의 산해진미
바다 내음 가득 품은 노랑조개회 맛은
잊을 수 없더라……

도솔암 가는 산책길을 걸으며
야생화 아름다운 산자락에
심어놓은 우리들의 이야기꽃은
가슴 깊은 곳간에 간직하고

니 다음에 하얀 서리 머리에 이고
지렁이 같은 굵은 주름 세월타고 넘을 적에
주막집 앉아서 대폿잔 기울이며
추억의 치맛자락을 들춰 보세나

Harvesting Beans

I planted black beans at the space of outskirts
In the sun power plant in Yeongam,
Where I have been working,
Thinking of my mother, who had sowed beans
Along the banks of the rice paddy and field to use even a little space.

Blooming pretty in violet color,
The beans bore fruit in Autumn.
The time I thrashed by a flail is bygones,
I harvested 10rice bags by a threshing machine of latest style.

Lim Won-sik/Korea

* Born at Haenam, Jeon-Nam, Korea.
* Graduated from Dept of Economics of Soongsil Univ. (B. E. Degree)
* Graduated from Graduate School of Administration of Jeon Nam Univ.(M. A. Degree)
* Graduated from Graduate School of Administration of Honam Univ. (Ph. D.)
* President of the Jeon Nam Newspaper.
* Visiting Prof. at College of Management of Honam Univ. & Inviting Prof. of Chosun Univ.
* Vice President of Spots Association of Jeon-Nam District(Present).
* President of Woori(Ltd.), N. S. T.(Ltd.), and Onnoori Taeyang-Kwang(Ltd.)
* A Letter of Citation for a Model Public Official. & A Medal of Nokjogeunjo, & The Order of National Service Merit(Dong Baek Jang).
* Great Award of the freedom Poets Association, &the Soongsil Men's Award.
* His Debut as an Essayist from the monthly "Essay Literature", the monthly "Literary Movement & Trend" as a Novelist and a Poet, and As a Critic from " the Monthly Literature".
* Published 'A Study of the Historical Literature on the Literary Art Published in Spring', 'Between the Law of Tax and the Consciousness' as Critical Essays.
* Collection of Columns: <Thinking in the Green Field>, <The Wind Blowing in Dream with other 3 vols.>
* A Collection of Essay: <The House where the Maples Grow>
* Poetical Anthologies: <The Rain of Spring Returning to the Secular Life with other 3 vols.>

The sun is not only a great help to the sun power plant,
But also gives a help in fruiting the beans,
And harvesting the beans like bounding stars
The amusement we share with neighbors,
Is bounding like a ball.

- Tr. by Won Eung-soon

콩을 거두며

내가 일하는
영암 태양광 발전소 주변의 빈터에
검은 콩을 심었다
한 평 땅도 놀리기 아까워
논둑 밭둑에 콩을 심던 어머님 생각에

보랏빛 꽃을 곱게 피우더니
가을 되어 열매가 익었다
도리깨로 타작하던 때는 옛일
최신식 콩 탈곡기를 돌려
열 가마니나 거둬들였다

햇볕은 태양광 발전뿐만 아니고
콩들도 잘 익혀 내는구나
통통통 별이 튀는 콩을 거둬
이웃들과 나누는 재미도
통통통

Helianthus Annus

- A Eulogy to the Late Kim Joung-woong, the President

O Love,
For Apollo, god of the Sun,

The ceaseless sewing sound of Christie,
A Water Sprite
At the classic room.

One day
Christie, the water sprite is pronounced
As incurable Thyroid Gland Cancer,

Her marching
Crossed the death river(Styx).

One day
When she turns once around 'Turning a Castle'
With stones on her head,
Her legs were cured,

No Jung-ai/Korea

* The date of my birth: November 5, 1938
* The university from which I graduated: Univ. of Joongang(Seoul, S. Korea)
* Major: Korean Language & Literature,
* Membership: The Literary Association for the International Poet & Poetress(S. Korea), The Literary Association for the Korean Race(S. Korea)
* Address : 142-8, Daehyun-dong, Seodaemun-gu, Seoul, 120-170, Korea

Turning twice,
The 'Moyang Castle'
Had made people recover from disease, and live long.

Hand in hand with Apollo
Taking a walk along the Moyang Castle path under the high and clear sky
She solicits earnestly her life,

With a mind
Taking care of Apollo's people
In the golden carriage.

Now we can see
The golden big flowers
Enclosing their stalks
With Large, lacerated petals,

And ripe seeds,
Conceived as flowers,

Now nearby,
We can see a hymn of joy
Beginning to hear.

- Tr. by Won Eung-soon

* Apollo, Christie: The names of Greece's mythology.

해바리기

-김 회장님의 성공기 축사

태양의 신 *아폴로를
사랑함이여.

고전방
물의 요정 *크리스티의
끊임없는 바느질 소리.

어느 날
물의 요정 크리스티의
갑상선암 선고,

죽음의 강을 건너온
행진곡.

돌을 머리에 이고
답성놀이 한 번 하면
다리 병이 낫고.

두 바퀴 돌면
무병장수 한다는
모양성(牟陽城)

아폴로 신과 손잡고
높고 맑은 하늘 모양성 길 산책하며
생명을 기구했음이며,

황금마차 속
아폴로 신의

백성들 하나하나를
챙기는 마음

톱니자국의 푸르고
커다란 잎사귀로 꽃대 감싼
황금빛 커다란 꽃

꽃으로 잉태한
알차게 여문 씨들

이젠 가까이에서
들려오기 시작한
환희의 송가도 보입니다.

* 그리스 신화에 나오는 신들의 이름

Mountains don't lay the Fault on Clouds

The mountain
Being patient,
Keeping silence,
And giving a new blood transfusion,

When we are worn out,
Are exhausted in soul,
Get lonesome,
And so feel somewhat sad,
Let's go the mountain.

The mountain
Gives us its vitality,
And the best tonic for our life.

Let's go the mountain, feeling somewhat melancholic,
With a broad smile on our face,
And go to the mountain welcoming us.

- Tr. by Won Eung-soon

Oh Jin-hwan / Korea

* Born in Suanbo in Chung-ju
* Graduated from Han-yang Univ., Dept. of Eng
* Graduated from the Dep of business administration of Yeon-se University
* Member of Korean Writer's Association
* Member of the International Association of Writers in Korea Headquarters
* Vice secretary general of the World Poetry Research Institute
* President of literary association 'An Annual Ring'
* Awarded the prize of the monthly magazine 'Literature 21'
* Awarded the prize of Tam-mee literature
* Awarded the prize of cultural exchange between India and Korea
* Awarded the Medal of Nokjoguenjeong
* Poetical Works: "A Persimmon left for Magpie" "In the bosom of you after becoming A Crane" etc.
* Literary Works: A commemorative work 'A fisherman who puts a bait for a man.
* Adrees: 2-202, Kyeongnam Apt, 1-8, Banpo-dong, Seocho-gu, Seoul, 137-765, Korea

산은 구름을 탓하지 않는다

침묵하며
인내하며
새로운 피를 수혈해 주는 산

일에 지쳤을 때
정신이 피로할 때
고독하다고 느껴질 때
왠지 서글퍼질 때
산으로 가자

산은
우리에게 활력과
생명 최고의 보약을 선물해 준다

왠지 우울하면 산으로 가자
마냥 미소 지으며
우리를 반겨 주는 산으로 가자

The Secret of the Portrait of the Warriors

From the wall, a thousand-year old war cry rises out of the dust
Haggard deer pant, horse hooves pound
The dirt of ancient Goguryeo flies high

Many ages have passed
Since the shooting star came to me
Fallen from an ancient time
The distant drumbeats pierce my heart

When the drum sounds
The mountain, resembling tiger stripes,
And the untamable field unite as one
The chased and the chaser in the game of life
The spilt blood of the sacrificed
The sweat of the hunter
Together, a ritual dance in the carnival

Park In-ae/Korea

* First debut as a poet through "Literary Movement & Trend"
* Debut as a poet through "he Third Literature"
* Debut as essay through "The Essay Literature and Art"
* A maneger of "The Third Literature"
* A Member of the Korean Writers' Association
* A Member of World Poetry Research Institude
* A Member of Literary Movement & Trend
* A Member of Korean Literature society of America
* A Member of Korean Literature society of Dallas
* Columnist of the News Korea
* E-mail: nadainae@naver.com

A bow drawn to full power
A dull arrow tip
Mercy flows from the eye of the warrior
No flutters stir the eye of the deer

Living shortens the distance to death
They stand up and run with shouts
Feet tangled in chaos
No fear in this last dance
Because they understand
Death is a part of life

Gazing upon this painting, full of irony
A rush of nostalgia springs for my own battles of the past
Those lives were sacrificed to protect this land
Here, the spirit of young Goguryeo is captured
The splendor of the antlers
Chains my ankles with grief
Captured by my thoughts, I stood
For a long while, immobile

수렵도의 비밀

벽에서 천년 묵은 함성이 먼지처럼 흩날렸다
사슴들의 거친 숨소리와 말발굽 소리
튀어 오르는 고구려의 흙

몇 광년의 시간을 통과하여
내게로 다가온 별똥별처럼
고대로부터 떨어져
심장에 박히는 먼 북소리

북소리가 울리면
호랑이 무늬를 닮은 산과
거친 들이 하나 되어
쫓고 쫓기는 한 판 사냥놀이
피 흘려 진설되는 희생도
놀이 같은 진설자의 땀방울도
어우러져 한 판 춤이 되는 사육제

힘껏 당긴 활시위
무딘 화살 촉
무사의 눈빛에서 흐르는 자애로움
사슴의 눈빛엔 흔들림이 없다

삶은 죽음과의 거리를 좁혀가는 것
일제히 일어나 소리치며 달려본다
어지러이 뒤엉킨 발과 발
마지막 춤사위가 두렵지 않음은
죽음이 삶의 한 편린이라는 것을

깨달았기 때문이다.

이 맹랑한 그림 앞에 서면
울컥 솟는 그리움
고구려를 지키다 스러져 간
젊은 무사의 혼백까지 담은 겐가!
화려한 뿔은
슬픈 발목을 잡고
상념은 박제가 되어
한참을 그 자리에 서 있었다

Ancient Women Are Alive

The two big rice kettles and the nickel silver pot
Are set up in the kitchen side by side,
And they makes a fire by dead branches into the fireplace.
Giving off red sparks,
The two big kettle's covers on the kitchen range
Puff off white steam fast like a steam engine train.
The rice in the kettle is cooked well
And the soup in the pot is boiled briskly.
This is a lovable sight of our traditional kitchen
Handed down from generation to generation
Which anyone could see in the villages of the country
And it must be a retrospective figure indulged in romantics and old memory,
Bearing comparison with the modern kitchen style.

On the days of 'Barley Hump' that means spring famine,
Our grandmothers, mothers, and sisters
Are now making a fire crouched
And heating our floors in the kitchen in my memoirs.

- Tr. by Won Eung-soon

Park Kwi-keun/Korea

* Born in Youngdong, Chungbuk, Korea
* While Serving in his Public Career for 20years
* Walking along the Poetic Lane by himself
* Wrote 108 Poems for 10days and 600 pieces of Poems for Etude in all.
* Mobile: 010-4723-5230/ E-mail: kksj0102@hanmail.net

옛 여인들은 살아 있다

큼지막한 가마솥 두 개와
양은솥 나란히 놓인 부엌 아궁이속
삭정이에 불이 지펴진다
시뻘건 불꽃이 삽시에 활활 타오르면
부뚜막 위 커다란 솥뚜껑 두 개가
기관열차 되어 허연 김을 모락모락 내뿜는다
밥솥에선 고슬고슬 밥이 익어가고
국솥에선 부글부글 국이 끓는다
시골마을 어디서나 흔히 볼 수 있던
대대로 이어온 재래식부엌의 정겨운 풍경이다
현대식 주방에 비해 뒤질 바 없는
예전의 낭만과 추억이 얼비치는 모습이다

가난에 힘겹던 보릿고개 시절
우리의 할머니, 어머니, 누나들은
지금도 내 기억 속에서 쪼그리고 앉아
군불을 때고 있다

Korea/Park Moon-jae

A Path Between White Birches

Clear water sound of this winter
Hearing from woods of white birches,
Is a cup of coffee in European deep brown color,
A sweet harmonious chord of Bach,
Or is the just one of Mozart.

A brilliant blossom of lilies
That I saw from a temple,
Could it be so fragrant
If man is suffered incessantly?

It's our mother's image of Chosun(Korea)
So benevolent,
Being delighted to see her young son
Just going back from the outdoors.

- Tr. by Won Eung-soon

Park Moon-jae/Korea

* Poet, Pen name: Jook Hyun
* Boarn at Seondu-ri, Munnae-myeon, Haenam-gun, Jeon-Nam, and brought up at Woosuyoung, Haenam.
* Completed Dept of literary Creative Literature, Art College, Jung-Ang Univ. and graduated from Dept. of Language Education, Graduate School of Education, Yon-Sei Univ.
* Retired as an ex-teacher of Middle & High School.
* Prize Winning Work as "Falling Snow" at a Literary Contest in Spring in the Kwangju Newspaper, 1963.
* Recommended as "Fog and 4 other Poems" in the monthly magazine "the Modern Poetry", 1980.* Published <Winter Orchard> as Children's Verse in "the Critical Children's Literature", 1981.* A Director of Yangpung Literary Men's Association, and A Vice Chairman of the Kangnam Men's Association.* A Member of the Literary Coterie 'Eung Si'.
* A Member of the Literary Men's Association of Korea; An Executive Committee of the Poets Association of Korea; A Chairman of the Reading Poems at Kangnam District.
* Received "Kosan Literature Award"; "Seaoul Great Literary Award"; "Young Rang Literature Award".
* Published the Poetical Anthologies entitled <Voice of the Winter Tree>, <Moran Day>, <An Abnormally Warm Winter>, <Sonnet of the Light of Grass>, <Passing by the Wood o White Birch>, and <Tamberly's Autumn> and <A Study of the Influence the Ballad Exerting on the Children's Rhyme> as a Critical Essay, etc.

자작나무 숲길

자작나무 숲에서 들리는
정결한 겨울 물소리
구라파풍(風)의 진갈색 커피 한 잔
바하의 감미로운 화음이거나
모짜르트의 그것이다.

한겨울, 산사(山寺)에서 본
눈부신 백합 한 송이
사람도 쉴새없이 달구면
저렇듯 향기로운가

이제 막, 마실 다녀온
어린 아들 반기시던
그윽히 자애로운
조선의 우리 어머니 상(像)이다.

The Ephemeral Existence 1

In this world
The saddest being
Is the sun.

Once in a day,
In crimson
You were born in scarlet,

Over the boundless sky,
Running toward,
One day desolate journey crying with tired,

You are the sad ephemeral being,
Who are entering into nirvana
In the declining,
Toward the western hill with melting into tears.

- Tr. by Won Eung-soon

Park Youn-ki/Korea

* Pen Name: Chosan.
* Born in Andong, Kyeongbuk, Korea
* Graduated from Cheonsong High School.
* First Debut as a Poet through "Literary Movement & Trend"
* Recorded as a Poet in "The Encyclopedia of Korean Poetry"
* A Member of the Association of Literary Movement & Trend.
* Address: 322-90 Chosan-ri, Habuk-myun, Yangsan City, Kyung-nam, Korea

하루살이 1

이 세상에서
가장 슬픈 하루살이는
태양이다

하루 한 번
붉게
붉게 울면서 태어나

구만 리
막막한 하룻길을
천지간 헤집으면 고달프게 울다가

서산머리에서
눈시울마저 붉힌 채
노을 속에 열반(涅槃)하는
슬픈 하루살이

The Wild Winter Passed

At last it has surely come!
The fine spring, vindicating its honor
Against the smart, hurt, and hard winter,

The sunshine burning hotly, hotly
Shines so dazzle our eyes there,
Look at the green mountain and green field.

Shaking out, shaking out,
Taking off winter rags,
Let's change into that new green clothes.

The lark chirps in the sky
The stream flows singing
In soft breeze caressing the frozen swelled ground,

Seo Jeong-nam/Korea

* A member of Korea writers' association
* A member of Korean modern poetry writers' association, a member of international pen club in Korea headquarters, second chairman of Seocho literary men's association, chairman of Chongda literary men's association, chairman of Korea psychology counsel association, an honorary Doctor of Literature and so on.
* A poet, a pastor, a judicial scrivener, a counselor of psychology and so on
* Address: 145-3,Docheongmyeon, Buangun, Jeon-Buk, Korea.

Let's run laughing, and climb up a green field,
Singing, and a high mountain,
The winter always has come and gone as it has ever been.

- Tr, by Won Eung-soon

그 광란의 겨울은 가고

마침내 오고야 마는구나!
쓰리고 아렸던 모진 겨울
설욕하는 화창한 새봄이

뜨겁게, 뜨겁게 꽃불 타오르는
햇살 부서져 눈이 부신 저기
푸른 산 푸른 들판을 보아라.

털어 버리고, 털어 버리고
겨울 누더기 벗어 버리고
하 푸른 새 옷을 갈아입자

종달새는 하늘에서 지저귀고
얼부푼 땅 애무하는 미풍에
시냇물도 노래하며 흐르나니

웃으면서 달려가자 푸른 들을
노래하며 올라보자 높은 산을
겨울은 항용 그리 오고 가나니

On Growing Old

Only the greenness is not fine,
As if the trees of the world grow old
And are more graceful,
The face with thick scums of time,
Or the growing old with lines of furrow of time,
Is also good.

Once
I had trembled from fear of browbeating,
Or I had fallen into trance at angular chisels,

But now
I have much in reserve
Treating anyone generously against the absurd things.

Shin Dong-myeong/Korea

* Born in Seoul
* Started a literary career through the magazine 'Literary Movement & Trend'(essay)
* Started a literary career through the magazine 'Literary 21'
* Member of the international Pen Club in Korea Headquarters
* Member of Korean Woman Writer's Association
* Member of Modern poetry association
* Member of Korean essayist Association
* Won the Kaya Gold Crown of the World Poetry, etc
* Published poetical works: The Will of Wings'. A Short and Long Story.
* Published literary jottlings: From Han River to Senue
* Stray notes: A Watercolor Painting in the Picture
* Address: 601, Hyundae Apt, 171-61, Bulgwang2-dong, Eunpyong-gu, Seoul, 123-042, Korea
* E-mail: sdm1445@hanmail.net

Rather than we are cheated by the flower
With our heart palpitates, being patient with smile silently
Turning his face, to be a man with generous chest,
Would be a blessing.

In order to bloom new leaves or flowers
As they would like to give up withered leaves or flowers,
Their dauntless attitude against the storms of life
Also should be fine.

That the end of the cliff,
Sometimes, which he should fly giving up his nest,
Being easy to fly when he gets light,
So throw away useless things,
Such a growing old would be good.

- Tr. by Won Eung-soon

늙는다는 건

푸르름만이 좋은 것은 아니야
세상의 나무들이 늙어서 더 아름다워지듯
세월의 더께가 겹겹이 쌓인 얼굴
시간의 이랑들 곳곳에 줄지어 선
늙음 또한 좋은 거야

한때,
객쩍은 으름장에 꽁꽁 언 동태가 된 적도
모난 정 맞고 맘 상한 적도 있지만
이제는
생뚱맞은 어이없는 일에도
껄껄 웃어 주는 여유가 생겼다니까

꽃에 속아 가슴 두근거리기 보담
돌아서서 수굿이 미솔 깨물 줄 아는
훈훈한 가슴이 된다는 건 축복인 거야

새 꽃 새 잎 피우기 위해
시든 꽃 시든 잎 내려놓듯
비바람에도 굽히지 않는 듬직함이라니

언젠가는 털고 날아가야 할
저 허공의 벼랑 끝
가벼울수록 날기 쉽기에
내려놓을 줄도 아는
늙음 또한 좋아진다니까.

The Reddened Sunset Behind a Forest

Along the path of maple trees
A grey-haired couple,
Passing or going ahead of one another in turn,
Are going to the mountain pass
Leaning on one another.
It's the end of autumn season,
A brace of yellow butterflies follow them,
The reddened sunset
Is spreading from the backside of a forest,
Carried on a wind
Blowing from somewhere.

- Tr. by Won Eung-soon

Shin Hae-sik/ Korea

* Born in Jeon-ju city, Jeonbuk, Korea.
* Graduated from Dept. of Korean Language for Teaching, & a Graduate School of Education, Jeonbuk Univ.
* Member of the Korean Writers' Association.
* Member of the Jeonbuk Writers' Association & of the Jeonbuk Poets' Association.
* Member of the Jeonbuk Pen Club.
* Vice President of the Jeonbuk Writers' Association.
* President of Jeonju Poong-mul Poets' Coterie.
* Vice Principle of Woon-am Middle School.
* First Debut as a new Poet from the Magazine, 'The Literary Movement & Trend', 1989.
* Poetical Anthology: 'Sonnets of Wangjeong-dong', 'The Reddened Sunset from the Backside of a Forest'.
* Address: #101-3 Soncheon-dong 1ga, Shin-il Apt.101-306, Jeonju City, Jeonbuk.

붉게 물든 노을이 숲 뒤쪽에서

단풍나무 숲길을 따라
백발의 부부가
앞서거니 뒤서거니
서로를 의지하며
산길을 가고 있다.
가을의 끝자락
노랑나비 한 쌍도 뒤를 따라가고
어디쯤에서 불어오는
바람에 날려
붉게 물든 노을이 숲 뒤쪽에서
번져오고 있다.

There's Time Tears Come To Our Eyes Blindly

In a day when we behold the sky by chance,
The scaled cloud is so brilliant
That there's time tears come to our eyes blindly.

The wounded words
That we are spitting out countlessly,
Are not only because of a stern authority.

When with you, time passes like a sweet music,
Without shaking by the instant desire,
We can look at you purely.

Though the shining moments
Simply
Are not 'Love',

In a day when we want to lean our heads on your shoulder,
With our words to say lost,
There's time tears come to our eyes blindly.

- Tr. by Won Eung-soon

Son Soon-ja / Korea

* Born at Pocheon, Geonggido.
* A Member of the Literary Men's Association of Korea.
* A Chairman of 'the Soyo Literature'.
* Received the Original Prize of the Space Poets Association of Korea.
* Received the Prize of Excellence of the Pure Literature.
* Poetical Anthology: <A Love Song of Soyo Mountain>.
* Collection of Essays: <A Happy Woman>.
* Address: 178-2, Sangyeon 1st-dong, 25 Setgolgil, Dongdoocheon, Geongigido, Korea.

무작정 눈물이 날 때가 있습니다

문득 하늘을 올려다 본 날
구름 비늘이 너무나 눈부셔
무작정 눈물이 날 때가 있습니다.

수 없이 뱉어 내는
상처의 말이,
서릿발 같은 위엄 때문이 아닙니다.

함께 있으면 시간이 달콤한 음악처럼 흐르고
순간의 욕망에 흔들리지 않고
순수하게 바라볼 수 있는 그대

그 빛나는 순간들이
그저,
사랑이 아니어도

할 말도 잊은 채
그 어깨에 머리를 기대고 싶은 날
무작정 눈물이 날 때가 있습니다.

Moving Is Power

He
Revived.

By energy
He moves,
The moving wave length
Comes closer,
Moving is power.

If the spinning top is dead, it stops,
If the bicycle's pedal stops, it falls down,
So if blowing wind stops, it disappears.

Climbing Mt. Bukhan, I saw
That trees and winds
All revived,
Moving.

- Tr. by Won Eung-soon

Tae Dong-chul / Korea

* Recommended As a Poet from the Literary Movement & Trend.
* A Member of the Literary Men's Association of Korea.
* Vice Chairman of the Guro Branch, of the Literary Men's Association of Korea.
* An Executive Secretary of the Academy of Literature.
* Address: 741-7, Oeri, Youngheungmyeon, Ongjingun, Incheon Metropolitan City, Korea.

움직임은 힘이다

그가
살아났다

에너지를 받아
움직인다
움직이는 파장이
바람으로 다가온다
움직임은 힘이다

팽이도 돌다 죽으면 멈춘다
자전거 페달 멈추면 쓰러진다
바람도 불다 멎으면 사라진다

북한산 오르다 보았다
나무들도 바람들도
움직이자
모두 살아났다.

An Ode to the Winter

Your horrified looks,
A branch of the tree in white snow
Like the subway in the dark tunnel,

In the closed window
The trembling white hands and feet
Are the patients anesthetized on the operating table,

The wandering salesman in the foreign land,
The cries of migrants bereft of friends
Under the chilly smiles.

The underground cafe
Welcoming the blank check and
Paving in a shroud as soft as carpets,

The raven's habit
Pecking darkness,
The dispersing dead carcasses all around,
And the burning beast of spring,
Alluring with a spring cold
Is the knocking, knocking sound drawing near to death.

- Tr. by Won Eung-soon

Won Eung-soon / Korea

* Graduated from Dept. of English Literature, Yonsei Univ.
* Poet, Ph.D. Emeritus Prof. of Kyung Hee Univ.
* Chief Editor of The Christian Literature of Korea(Quarterly Magazine)
* Manager & Editor of the Professor's Newspaper
* Elder of Dongsoong Presbyterian Church

겨울 송가

섬뜩한 그대 모습
하얀 눈 속의 나뭇가지
어두운 터널 속의 지하철,

닫힌 창문 속
하늘거리는 하얀 손과 발
수술대 위에 마취된 환자들,

차가운 미소 속에
외지에서 방황하는 외판원
친구 잃은 철새의 울음소리.

백지수표를
환대하는 지하카페
수의로 포장된 융단 같은

어둠을 쪼는
갈 까마귀의 습성
흩어지는 시체들
꽃샘으로 유혹하는
불타는 봄 짐승
죽음으로 다가오는 노크소리, 노크소리.

A Cuckoo In Autumn

In spring season
The foolish cuckoo,
Who doesn't know for the spring to pass,
And its yearning, cuckooes cuckoo
In spite of autumn,
And sheds bitter tears from your throat.

Spring has passed and summer also gone,
Like a cyclonic wind all things have gone,
But after it has come at the end of the season of the blazing twilight
Only your longing seems to be in flame
In your throat.

Cuckoo, Cuckoo, Cuckoo---

Over the empty space
Only the white clouds
Float away without response.

- Tr. by Won Eung-soon

Yeo Han-kyung/Korea

*Born in Munkeong, Keongbuk
*Graduated in Korean literature from Andong National University, Yeongnam University
* Resigned from a teacher at Cheonggu high school in Daigu
*Decorated with an national medal and a presidential citation
* Member of the Korean Writers' Association
* Committee of the Korean Headquarter at International Pen Club
- Daegu Regional Board(Vice President, Consultant)
* Modern Poets Association of Korea(Trustee, Committee for Development)
*Published several books
*Address: 505, wubang town 5dong, 240, hwanggeum 1dong, suseong-gu, Daegu city

가을의 뻐꾸기

봄에는
봄 가는 줄도 모르고
그리움도 모르던 멍청이 뻐꾸기가
가을에서야 뻐꾹뻐꾹
너의 목에선
피가 마른다

봄이 가고 여름이 가고 회오리치듯
모두가 가버렸건만
노을이 불타는 계절의 가지 끝에서야
너의 목에선
그리움이 불타나 보다

뻐꾹 뻐꾹 뻐꾹……

대답 없는 허공엔
흰 구름만
떠나고

The Rebellion of an Egg

The eggs that we sold them at the rural market(opening at every 5 days) and bought our necessities of life, and that my grandmother should request me to take them out to her, when the hen clucked to lay. Then, again after the hen grew bigger as a brood hen, the eggs that she laid, making only one hole by a needle, sucking its white part somewhat conscientiously, and inhaling at a time its shaking yellow one carefully, with a throbbing heart.

At every time the volcano's sulfur spring blazes up thrusting through the thick surface of the oval earth, I think of the hen's egg. Again I ponder over a degree of the egg's angle, after its yellow part comes out of the weakest shell, when its soul revolves and rotates, Each time its yellow chicken's neck sticks out, like the fear of sulfurous fire spreading on the white surface, feeling the heart's beating in the earth.

Yoo Hee-bong/Korea

* Recommended as a Poet from the 'Hyundae Poetry' in 1993.
* Poetic Anthology: Published 6 books with 'the Flower of Language'.
* Essay Collection: 'The Happy Spring Well'.
* Art of Writing Creative Poetry: 'To Create Poetry Is To Write Future'.
* Director of Poetry in National Movement Center of Clean Contents, Korea.
* Present: Lecturer of Hoseo Univ., Suwon Univ.(Ph. D. of Business Management).
* Tel: 02-6412-0702/ 010-6412-0702

O! I know, a dot or a stroke in the sentence of the Bible cannot be added or subtracted as "next the last judgement should be done by fire" Over the east sea at Kobe, Japan, there happened a serious uproar by revolt of fire threatening thousands of lives. Ah! Should I swallow a bitter cup tonight? A pile of unfertilized eggs in the street, broken, even a valuable life shaking like automobiles.

Looking at the digging scene of the hot spring in my home town, I think, I had taken eggs out from a small hole at my childhood. With the poor people's sighs in the Great Wall of China, seen through the window of the space capsule, the revolt of the egg's yellow part streamed out by the shake of the earth's axis, I think.

- Tr. by Won Eung-soon

계란의 반란

시골 오일장에 내다 팔아 가족의 필수품 사오곤 했던 계란, 닭장 안 암탉 소리 울면 할무이 어김없이 꺼내 오라는 닭의 알, 다시 씨암탉이 돼 낳은 닭의 알, 장바구니 속 꼭 하나만 바늘구멍 내 흰 살 약간 양심적으로 빨다 가슴 두근두근 노른자 출렁출렁하니, 조심스럽게 쭉-쭈우욱 힘겹게 흡입한 닭의 알.

타원형의 지구 두꺼운 지표를 뚫고 유황불 솟구칠 때마다, 그 닭의 알을 생각한다 노른자가 나온 후 극히 빈약한 껍질 속 생명의 혼 공전과 자전을 할 때 계란의 각도를 생각한다 하얀 표면 번지던 유황불의 두려움처럼 노오란 병아리 목 내밀 때마다 심장이 뛰는 지구의 박동음

오! 일 점 일 획도 가감이 없다는 성경 구절" 다음에는 꼭 불로써 심판이 있으리라" 바다 건너 고베에는 수천의 생명 불의 반란 때문에 큰 난리가 일어났다 아! 오늘밤 마음의 고배(苦杯)라도 들어야 할까 한 줄 한 알의 생명이 자동차처럼 흔들리다 깨져 버린 무정란의 달걀 더미.

내 고향 온천을 파낼 때, 어린 시절 바늘구멍으로 퍼내던 달걀을 생각한다 빗나간 계란의 각도를 느껴 본다 우주선에서도 보인다는 만리장성 민초들의 한숨 속에, 지구의 무게 축이 흔들려 흘러나온 노른자 계란의 반란을 생각한다 나는.

What Do You Call Me?

I walk into a wood.
The unknown grasses wave.
In a moment I am going to exchange looks
With a single grass, staggering to keep its balance,
The wind passes quickly shaking the grasses.

The wavering grasses!
What do you call me?
The grasses, that you have seen me to fall often over the hill,
I stumble over your green totter!
I am a beast who can break off your neck.

The curving flower stalk with flowers like a needle!
After you've suffer from illness catching an end of winds through
all night,
You made a flower petal bloom!
The wavering grasses exposing their own old season,
The whipping marks on your calf of legs are dark green.

Yoo Hee-Jeong/Korea

* Pen name: Yu Anna
* Born at Gochang, Jeonbuk, Korea
* Recommended as a poet in the Literary Magazine 'Aejee'
* Studied at F.I.T. New York Fashion School
* Finished Specialist Course on the Creative Writing of Jung-ang Univ.
* Address: Umyeon-dong, Seocho-Gu, Daelim Apt. 101-402 Seoul, Korea
* H.P: 010-7147-6096 / E-mail: annaryoo@naver.com

One day, the grasses, which have come rushing into black clouds
Like a child getting chased at the cracks of thunder,
What should I call you?
O the grasses, swaying and fading after blooming a few days!
O the flower petal, flowing between twilight I underlined them.

- Tr. by Won Eung-soon

너는 나를 무엇이라 부르는가

숲 속을 걷는다
이름 모를 풀이 흔들린다
애써 균형을 잡으며 비틀거리는 풀잎 하나와
눈 맞추려는 순간 바람이 그 풀을 휙 흔들고 지나간다

흔들리는 풀이여
너는 나를 무엇이라 부르는가
내가 자주 넘어지던 고갯마루를 보았을 풀이여
네 푸르른 흔들림에 내 발 걸려 넘어지는 구나
나는 네 목을 꺾을 수도 있는 짐승이다

바늘 같은 꽃을 달고 자꾸 휘어지는 몸이여
거친 바람 한 끝을 움켜쥔 채 밤 새 신열 앓다
꽃잎 피워 냈구나
옛 시절을 들춰내며 자꾸 흔들리는 풀이여
종아리에 채찍 자국 검푸르다

어느 날 천둥소리에 쫓기던 아이처럼
먹구름 속을 달려왔을 풀이여
나는 너를 무어라 불러야 하는가
한 사흘 피어 흔들리다 지고 마는 풀이여
내가 밑줄 친 황혼 사이로 흘러가는 꽃잎이여

The Spring of Gangjin

O, sloppy painters! painting with water colors,
Don't argue about the colors at random
In the field of Gangjin, a part of the southern land.

The *pink flowers, blooming splendidly at the rice paddy fields,
And the yellow flowers, coming out in groups
At the paddy field and the dry field here and there,

And azaleas, golden bells, and the camellias blooming
With their own beautiful figures at the foot of the mountain hills,
Having a distant view on them out of the bus windows together with exclamation,

When we look over Ganjin bay from the Cheonilgak,
Dasan thached cottage at Mt. Mandeok, for Chilryang or Maryang of Daegu,
We are united as a state of objects and subject.
Yes, it's right. The spring of Gangjin among four seasons,
Is the best beautiful present of nature God has given us.

- Tr. by Won Eung-soon

* It means 'Astragalus Sinicusl.'

Yoon Hyoung-soon / Korea

* Born at Daegu-myun, Kangjin-gun, Jeon-Nam, Korea
* Graduated from College of Agriculture, Jeon-Nam University
* Served at Ministry office of Agriculture for 20 Years, and at National Agrecultural Co-operation Federation for 13 Years
* Manager of the Kindred Society of the Haenam Family "Yun"
* Received the Prize in Literary Contest for Poetry under the Auspices of Jeonnam Daily Newspaer(1965)
* Member of the World Poetry Institute
* Address : Hyundae Prime Apt. 207-501, Sinjeong-maeul, 2-dong, Pungdeokcheon, Suji-gu, Yongin City, Gyeonggi-do, Korea

강진(康津)의 봄

수채화를 그리는 어설픈 화백들이여
남녘의 땅 강진의 봄 들판에서
색깔에 대하여 함부로 논하지 말지어다.

논바닥에 흐드러지게 피어 있는 연분홍의 자운영꽃이며
논두렁 밭두렁 여기저기 군데군데 무리 지어 피어 있는
노랑물결의 유채꽃 하며

야산발치 산자락에 화사한 자태를 뽐내며 피어 있는
진달래 개나리 동백꽃들을 달리는 차창으로
관조(觀照)해 보면 감탄사가 절로 나고

만덕산 다산초당 천일각에서 칠량 대구 마량쪽의
강진만을 내려다보면 물아일체(物我一體)의
경지에 빠지게 된다
그렇습니다 사계절 중 강진의 봄은 하늘이 내려주신
가장 아름다운 자연의 선물입니다.

Same Mountain, Same Poem

There is only one mountain left, with a heaven
Between the heaven and earth, with the sun shining,
The green winds spreading out, with all my heart,
And left only one poem for me not to aspire
In high, right, and happy world of dream.

The worship for machinery, snatched the love's meaning
Black pollution, uneasy earth for the weather caprice,
Turning and turning in the checkered windings of the years,
Now finally makes me return to one mountain, and one poem.

Aspiration for the true life acting with an imposing air,
Recognizing the secret of my deep being with wisdom of a clear life,

---

Yoon Sang-hyun/Korea

* Pen name: Hyo-won(曉苑)
* Date of Birth: 1930. 1.30.
* Born at Gyul-dong, Doam-myeon, Gangjin-gun, Jeonnam, Korea.
* Founded the Dooryun Literary Circle(1959)
* Member of a Literary Coterie "Han-deum" magazine(1972)
* Member of the Korean Writers' Association(1973)
* Recommended as a Poet in the Weekly Literary Magazine, "the Hankook Poetry"
* Awarded a Great Prize of "the Hankook Poetry"(2005) and received the prize of Nosan Literature.(2010)
* President of the Hankook Literary Club(Present)
* Publication: "The Vein"(1960), "A Summer Dream in the Green Field"(1970), "The Original Home"(1999), "The Poetical Anthology of Yoon Sang-hyun"(2013)
*Address: 713 Sungsa-dong, e-Pyeonhan-Sesang 117-1301, Deokyang-gu, Goyang City, Kyunggi-do

Filling with a silent mountain, I will return to my native place.
Singing a clear poem, I will stay at my own home

In vacant spirit against spider's web of time
Being a more beautiful person than a star,
Singing a happier song than a bird...
The moon waxes as if when does it wane,
The sun rises anew to the sky as if when does it set down.

- Tr. by Won Eung-soon

여산 여시(如山 如詩)

천지간에 하늘이 있는, 햇빛이 열리는
초록바람이 번지는, 산(山) 하나만 남았네.
일구월심, 높고 바르고 기쁜 꿈자리로
더 바랄 게 없는 시(詩) 하나만 남았네.

사랑의 의미를 앗아간 기계 바람이며
검은 오염, 기후변화에 흔들리는 지구.
세월의 기구한 굴곡 속에 돌고 돌아온 이 자리에
이제, 山 하나로, 詩 하나로 부족함이 없네.

꿀리지 않고 만들어가는 진실한 목숨의 희구 속에
깊은 존재의 비밀을 알고 맑은 삶의 지혜를 지니며
정한(靜閑)한 산으로 채우고, 나의 본가(本家)에 들어 있겠네
청정(淸淨)한 시로 노래하고, 나의 본가(本家)에 머물러 있겠네

시대의 혼미환 거미줄에 비운 마음으로
별보다 아름다운 사람, 새보다 즐거운 노래……
언제 기울였느냐는 듯이 달이 차 오르네
언제 흘렀느냐는 듯이 해가 새로이 솟네.

Delight

We are so much joyful
To meet each other.
Blooming the smiling flowers
In delight beyond our endurance,

Our piled-up talks
Are very so emotional,
Though we've none to say more,
The stories are endless as a legend.

Saying it's time to go,
But hesitating again,
We surprise at a long hour like an instant,
Constantly having unsatisfied feeling.

Leaving in haste,
But the unforgettable stream in whispers
And the mottled shade of smiling colors
Made us in feeling an irresistible yearning for.

- Tr. by Won Eung-soon

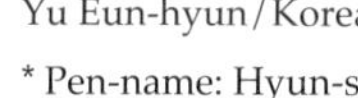

Yu Eun-hyun / Korea

* Pen-name: Hyun-san * Born in Incheon metropolitan city
* Graduated from Dongkook University(economics)
* Started literary career through 'Dongyang Literature'
* Member of Korea free poetry poet association * Member of Academic Society of National Ethics(Present)* Member of the Literary Society of Korean Writers(Present) * Member of the Buddhist Priest's Union of Korea(Present)
* Occupied the professor of the National Police College * Won the order of nokjo geunjeong * Published a collection of poems entitled 'There is a Mountain, so the trees', 'Along the Mountain and River'
* Address: 215-8, Juan1-dong, Nam-gu, Incheon metropolitan city, Korea

환희(歡喜)

서로 만나면
온 몸으로 반가워라
가슴 벅찬 기쁨에
고운 웃음꽃 활짝 피어나

밀렸던 이야기
더 없이 정겨워서
하고픈 말 따로 없이도
끝없는 이야기는 전설이 되어

이젠 가야지 하면서도
또 머뭇거리고
순간이듯 기~ㄴ 시간에 놀라
끝내 아쉬움 못내 새기며

서둘러 떠났어도
떠나지 않는 여울소리에
아롱진 웃음빛 그늘 속엔
환희 벅찬 그리움 솟구처

Dokdo Island

Dokdo Island!
Many days passed quickly,
And the moment taking your first step,
From your deep blue body,
The wind like a legend raised quickly
And my legs staggered.

You embrace the sea and the heaven in your arms,
And stand in the brave figure,
Stopping in an immense period.

You're a guardian angel of our land
Holding the sun of fireball in your bosom,
Burning your pain up alone,

Hold your tongue,
Until the day the distorted history

Yun Su-a / Korea

* Born at Chon-An, Chung-Nam, Korea.
* A Reciter of Poetry
* Recommended as an essayist winning the prize
* Editorial staff of magazine Jigumunhak('98 ~'01) & Chief of Administration of "World Poetry Institute"
* Meantime, Chief of Administration of "Korean Literature Institute"
* President of Sihyang Poets' club
* Address : 115-902, Hyundae HillState, 155, Onsudong, Gurogu, Seoul, Korea

Will be proved true.

O, Dokdo Island!
The last chastity of this continent .

- Tr. by Won Eung-soon

독도

독도여!
숱한 날들 달려와
첫발자국 내딛는 순간
너의 짙푸른 몸뚱어리에서
전설 같은 바람이 솟구치고
나의 다리는 휘청거렸다.

바다와 하늘을 한몸에 품고
억겁의 시간 속에 멈춰 선
용맹한 자태

불덩이 태양을 온몸으로 끌어안고
홀로 아픔을 사르는
국토의 당돌한 수호신

차라리 침묵하거라
왜곡의 역사가
진실로 귀결되는 그날까지

대륙의 마지막 정절
독도여!

The Immortal Soul

The cursed and ruthless Death
Has robbed a noble son
M.G.R. is no more
The early hours of December 24, 1987
Echoed the tragic news
Of the sudden demise of M.G.R.

Tamil Nadu went bersek with grief
Many died of shock
Some burnt themselves as a gesture of loyalty
Many were saved from committing suicide
Women wailed and mourned
Their grief knew no bounds

Three million turned up for funeral
Some were trampled to death
The desperate police opened fine
Some nourners died in vain
Madras was torn by riots
The ruthless damage shocked the world

G. Soosai/Malaysia

Prof. Dr. G. Soosai
Sebastian Villa
73, Talan Patani
10150 Penang Malaysia

불멸의 영혼

저주스럽고 무례한 죽음이
고귀한 아들을 강탈했다
각하는 더 이상 각하가 아니다
1987년 12월 24일 이른 시각
각하의 급격한 서거의 슬픈 소식이 메아리쳤다

타밀나두는 슬픔으로 휩싸였다
많은 사람들이 충격으로 죽었고
몇 명은 충성의 몸짓으로 분신했다
많은 사람들이 자살을 해서 구원받았다
여인들은 통곡하며 울었고
그들의 슬픔은 한이 없었다

삼백만 인파가 장례에 왔고
몇은 밟혀 죽었다
절박한 경찰은 총을 쏘았고
몇은 허무하게 죽어갔다
마드라市는 총으로 찢겨졌고
잔인한 손상은 세계를 경악시켰다

The Cuckoo

Each year it comes, this bird from far away--
The welcome call-- "cuckoo" we hear it say;
And not in "flock" or "bevy", "cast" or "fall,"
But one alone, or two, and that is all.

No problem, housing, does the female find--
A sparrow's nest? the cuckoo does not mind!
She alys her egg, it matters little where,
And leaves to match with those already there.

To feed her young-- this, too, no problem gives.
The birds deceived will see the stranger lives;
He quickly grows, the nest becomes too small,
So he evicts those "legal tenants" all;

The "squatting" cuckoo thus for board and bed
Has naught to pay and with the best is fed;
So Spring is here-- "in April come he will"
And birds and beasts all God's decress fulfill;

In August, to that other clime he goes--
The "best of both"-- and this the cuckoo knows!

J. Cullen/N. Ireland

82 Knockvale Park
Belfast BT5 6HJ
N. Ireland

뻐꾸기

매년 이 새는 멀리서 온다.
환영의 소리 - "뻐꾹", 우린 그게 뭔지를 듣는다.
그리고 무리로 몰리지도, 비상하지도, 내려앉지도 않고
홀로, 혹은 둘이서 온다 - 그게 전부다.

암컷은 아무 문제도, 집도 찾지 않는다.
참새의 둥지? 뻐꾸기는 걱정 않는다.
그녀는 알을 낳고, 장소 때문에 걱정 않는다.
그리고는 이미 거기 있던 동료들과 어울리기 위해 떠난다.

자식을 먹이는 것 - 이 또한 문제가 없다.
그들은 이방인들이 자기 삶을 보는 것을 속인다.
그는 매우 빨리 자라며 둥지는 적어지게 된다.
그래서 그는 법적인 전세인들 모두를 추방시킨다.

그래서 식탁과 침대를 찾게 되는 움츠린 뻐꾸기는
방세를 지불하는 것관 무관하게 좋은 먹이로 먹혀진다.
그래서 봄이 있다 - "4월이면 그는 올 것이고……"
그리고 새와 모든 동물은 신의 섭리를 완성한다.

8월이 되어, 계절이 바뀌면 그는 간다.
양쪽에게 있어서의 최선책 - 그리고 뻐꾸기는 그것을 안다.

My Name

My name
I was told since I was very little
means "felicidad"
You should be happy, sabes?
We come to live on Earth!
Our body
produces a few flowers
as the herbs do.
Happiness: "Felicidad"
a star for us.

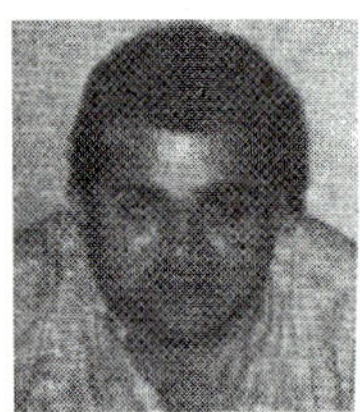

Daniel De Culla/Spain

POBox 2117
09080-Burgos-Spain

나의 이름

내가 아주 어렸을 적부터
들어오던 나의 이름은
너는 행복해야 한다는 뜻의
"felicidad"를 의미한다.
우리는 지구 위에 살기 위해 오지 않았던가!
우리의 육체는
숲이 그렇듯이
조금의 꽃들을 만들어낸다.
행복, 그 이름 "felicidad"
별이 우릴 위해 있다.

Apocalypse

My world dissolves itself at sunset.
In front of my eyes a procession
of dead friends and distant enemies
now indifferent to all polemic ideas.

Oh! How conceited and arrogant
I have been throughout my youth,
daring to foretell the arrival
of the knights of the Apocalypse,
and the dust of the stars
becoming rocks of the roads!

My eyes are sick of loving,
and from my name the blood flows.
When the moon of solitude comes,
I remain hungry and sleepy
among the tigers of the night
while time and passion
take me in their arms forever.

Teresinka Pereira / U.S.A.

* Dr. Teresinka Pereira, President of IWA
* Member of the American Civil Liberties Union
* Member of the Council for Secular Humanism
* Member of the United Nations Assoc. USA and the Business Council for the United Nations Ambassador at Large of the International States Parliament for Safety and Peace IWA Representative at Unesco: Emeritus Dr. Francis Dessart IWA Ambassador at UNESCO and UN: Dr. Jorge Alberto Costa e Silva
* Address : P.O.Box 352048 Toledo, OH 43635-2048, U.S.A.
* E-mail: tpereira@buckeye-express.com

SOME TIMES

Some times nothing matters.
I don't care for the twinkle
of the stars or the sunshine.

Some times not even the poem
matters, when I feel dialocated
in myself, incapable of forgiving...

My tongue, in whatever language
I try, sounds like the wind
that does not know where
it will end up today...

My voice does not reach
the distance in which
you placed my fault.

Silence cuts my desire
like a fine steel blade.

세계시문학 제31집 (2013)

인쇄 2013 년 11 월 25 일
발행 2013 년 11 월 29 일

편저자 | 정송전
펴낸이 | 김효열
역 자 | 원응순
편집부장 | 김경희
편 집 | 이미정
마케팅 | 김효숙 · 김영미

펴낸곳 | **을지출판공사**

등록번호 · 제 2-741 호
등록일자 · 1985 년 2 월 14 일
주 소 · 서울시 마포구 서교동 394-81 홍익B/D 3층
우편번호 · 121-840
전 화 · 02) 334-4050
팩시밀리 · 02) 334-4010
E-mail : ejp4050@hanmail.net

값 20, 000원

ISBN 978-89-7566-147-1 03810

세계시문학회
서울시 마포구 서교동 394-81 301호
☎ 02-334-4050, 019-234-8416 · 010-8747-4050
120-840